A Faith Wo

A Church Worth Joining?

For Douglas.

with our love & prayers

+ Jim ~ Cyril.

A Faith Worth Sharing?

A Church Worth Joining?

CYRIL ASHTON AND JACK NICHOLLS

Foreword by Alan Chesters

DARTON·LONGMAN + TODD

First published in 1995 by
Darton, Longman and Todd Ltd
1 Spencer Court
140–142 Wandsworth High Street
London SW18 4JJ

ISBN 0–232–52027–5

A catalogue record for this book is available
from the British Library

The Scripture quotations in this publication are taken from *The New
International Version* published and coypright 1973, 1978 and 1984 by
International Bible Society.

Phototypeset by Intype, London

Printed and bound in Great Britain by
Redwood Books, Trowbridge

*To the clergy and people of the diocese
of Blackburn, with great affection.*

Contents

Foreword

For a Church that needs all the encouragement it can get, Canon Cyril Ashton and Bishop Jack Nicholls are encouragers. Their combined experience, both inside and outside the diocese of Blackburn, has been forged on the anvil of realism in a Church which faces many serious challenges to its continuing life. They see the Church as it is, but consistently present a vision of the Church as it can be. In an age when there are many prophets of doom, it is very good to be able to work with people who speak and write positively about the Christian community, and who expect the Holy Spirit to continue to work in and through it. Both authors are aware of the weaknesses of the Church, and of the pressures upon it; nevertheless, their message is one of hope. They address perceptively some of the issues it faces and are enthusiastic about the opportunities that lie before it.

Although this book has emerged from their thinking and working together during the Decade of Evangelism, its roots go much deeper than that. Their separate vocations, although traced through distinctive strands of spirituality, show a heartening convergence of understanding and purpose. It is a refreshing sign of hope. I stand with the authors in wholeheartedly declaring that we do have a faith worth sharing, and, given our dependence on the grace of God, a Church worth joining. I hope many people will read this book, especially clergy, ministers and the lay readers in the Church. I warmly commend it, and happily send it on its mission of love, encouragement and challenge, with my prayers and good wishes.

ALAN CHESTERS
Bishop of Blackburn

Preface

This book has been written by two people, one the Bishop of Lancaster, the other the Director of Training for the diocese of Blackburn. It has emerged out of work that we have been doing together, with teams of both clergy and laity, in the Blackburn diocese. We come from entirely different backgrounds, one a raving Catholic (J.N.) and the other a sensible Charismatic Evangelical (C.A.). We speak about things we know to be true, that we have worked through for ourselves. Both of us have had considerable parish experience, and have reflected long on the things we write about. Our styles are different, sometimes markedly so, but we have one message. God is renewing his Church, and everyone has a part to play in this. Our heart's desire is to see the Church we both love growing in the way we know is possible. This inevitably means that we need to take stock, not only of our human resources, but also of the resources so freely and generously given by the Holy Spirit.

Our conviction is, of course, that our faith is worth sharing, and our Church is worth joining, but we recognise the need for much love and encouragement in order to build the confidence of Christians in these two realities. We have written with the Church of England in mind, but we hope that there is much that can be shared with other Christian communities, because we have so much in common. Both of us record with great gratitude the gift of Christians from diverse traditions, who have shaped and formed our spirituality. The book is aimed at leaders, clergy and PCC members, homegroup leaders, and all Christians who want to work through the issues involved in creating a climate for healthy growth. The appendices take the form of a DIY section, especially the discipleship course, 'We Believe', based on the Nicene Creed. We have found this simple course enormously valuable in our own diocese, and offer it with love.

From beginning to end our message is one of hope. We know that God has great power, and we know something of the vast reservoirs of goodwill, faith and commitment that exist in the Church. We want to encourage Christians to put these things together, so that the Church will move forward with confidence. Someone once said, 'If you don't know where you are going, you will end up somewhere else.' We hope this book will inspire Christians with fresh vision for their Church, giving new direction, and providing practical help to turn vision into reality.

Acknowledgements

We are grateful to a number of people for the help they have given us in preparing this book. Beryl Kilpatrick, Bishop Jack's secretary, cheerfully did most of his typing and acted as minder when he was trying to write. Many thanks also to Clare and Rachel Nicholls who did lots of photocopying. Christine Ellis and Jayne Earnshaw helped to prepare the course 'We Believe', for inclusion in the appendix. John Binks, Peter Hopwood, Rujon Morrison, David Gray and Margaret Baxter were responsible for writing and revising the course called 'We Believe' (Appendix 1). Appendix 2 was prepared by Peter Hopwood. It has to be said that their enthusiasm for their task has provided much inspiration and impetus for groups within our parishes. David Carroll has good-naturedly read the text and made many valuable observations; we are thankful for his combination of friendship and skill. Morag Reeve, our editor at DLT, has demonstrated many of the qualities of Christian love we write about. She is constantly supportive and encouraging, always ready with helpful suggestions, and patient when we have failed to meet deadlines.

Introduction

Freda is quite a character. Five feet tall, sixty-something years old, bouncing with life and full of fun. She looks quite ordinary, but God doesn't look on outward appearances, he looks on the heart, and she is very special underneath. Freda has four sons; her husband had a tumour on the brain which caused a long period of illness through which she nursed him. One of her sons has been in serious trouble with the police. This, and many other things, built up a catalogue of disasters for Freda. Recently, she went on a ten-day out-of-doors retreat in North Wales as part of her annual holiday. Each day the retreatants were taken out for a long walk to a pre-arranged spot and were given a view on which to meditate. All went well while the weather held good, but one day the heavens opened. 'Surely', she thought, 'we won't go out today' – but they did. Soaked to the skin they trudged up a mountainside to a slate quarry and were told to meditate on a slag-heap. 'I must be bloody mad', she thought to herself as she sat uncomfortably peering at the slag-heap. But as she waited she began to think of her own life, scarred just like the slag-heap, hopeless, depressed and in pain. As she reflected, looking on the rain-soaked desolation in front of her, she caught sight of a lovely wild flower pushing its way through the waste, and it gave her hope. She thought to herself, 'If I stayed here long enough the whole slag-heap would become a glory of wild flowers.' It was, for Freda, an experience of resurrection.

God was with Freda, he waited for her at the place of dereliction and revealed the richness and beauty that exists even in the most depressing human situations.

Our aim in the Decade of Evangelism is to remove the veil from people's eyes so they can recognise the God who is already there. The Church often acts as though it possessed Jesus, behaving as his 'minder', and being willing to share him with others only if they live up to standards set by itself. When people come up to us with the request the Greeks put to Philip, 'Sir, we would see Jesus', we must not offer them a rule-book but a relationship. Above all, we offer a relationship in which Jesus delights to meet with people just as they are, 'warts and all'. The Church must not get in the way, preventing people seeing Jesus by insisting that they look through our spectacles which are heavily discoloured by our own particular cultural and religious interpretations. We must give them a clear view.

In the light of this, two very important questions need to be thoughtfully considered: is my faith worth sharing? and, is my Church worth joining? Since its beginning the Church has grown because Christians have wanted to share both their faith, and their Church, with others. The twentieth century has seen a marked decline in confidence, with many Christians appearing uncertain about their faith, and not at all sure that their friends would want to be part of their Church. There is, in fact, a reality-gap between what we profess to believe, and what we can with confidence claim. The vocabulary of transformation which is used of the Christian faith in Scripture, in the liturgy and hymns of the Church, and in the rhetoric of evangelists, serves often to fill us with shame and embarrassment, because it reminds us of what is missing. Similarly, when we think of the Church, what we have at the local level is not the welcoming, attractive, challenging community the New Testament describes, but so often a rather limpid, chaotic, confused group of people, who always seem to be fighting about the most trivial things. The unfortunate experience of many is that the Church has become a rather exclusive and defensive religious organisation, closed to all but the fiercely resolute, and unable to open its doors to those who most need Christ.

Not surprisingly, therefore, the task before us in the Decade of Evangelism is to do with theology and ecclesiology. It is theological in that we must get a clearer picture of the nature of God, and it is ecclesiological in that we must get a clearer picture of the nature of the Church. As we do this we believe that Christians will be able to speak with greater confidence about their faith, and will be able to invite their friends into their Church without apology or embarrassment.

It is our hope that soon we will be able to drop the title, 'the Decade of Evangelism', as the thinking of the whole Church shifts from seeing faith as a private matter to seeing it as something that can be joyfully shared; and from seeing the Church as being a private club to seeing it as being rightly open to all. In any event, this book is written as an encouragement to move in this direction, and it is written with a profound, though often uncomfortable, love for the Church.

1

Knowing God

The question is not, how can I know *about* God but how can I know God? Knowing about God is difficult enough, libraries have been written about God. Knowing God, however, is much easier and yet at the same time more demanding. In the Old Testament, one of the meanings of the word 'knowing' is 'being intimate with' or 'having intercourse with'. So when we are told for example that David 'knew' Bathsheba it meant considerably more than that they were just good friends! So it is with knowing God. How can we be so close to God that only the most intimate language of love can begin to describe our relationship with him? For Christians the answer is simple yet profound: 'through Jesus Christ our Lord'. What is more, if you want to know what God is like you must look to Jesus for, as Bishop Michael Ramsey says, 'In God there is no un-Christlikeness at all'. So let us look at Jesus.

There is a story, supposedly true, about a little boy called Richard who, when he was about seven years old, moved house with his parents to a new area. His parents were concerned as to how well he would settle into a new school, but they need not have worried as he soon made friends and began to bring them home after school. However, after only a very short time his friends stopped coming home with him and so his father asked why this was. The little boy made no reply and so his father asked him, 'Richard, is it because of your mother?' It was.

'Richard, is it because of your mother's hands?' It was, for his mother's hands were unbearable to look at. They were disfigured to the point of being almost unrecognisable, they were monstrous. Richard was ashamed of his mother's hands. And so his father told him this story. When Richard's mother was young she worked as a make-up demonstrator in a large store. She needed to have, and had, beautiful hands. Then she met Richard's father, they fell in love and married. Eventually Richard came along and his mother stopped working in the large store in order to look after Richard. One day, when he was about two years old, his mother heard an awful scream from the other room as she sat in the kitchen. She ran in and found that Richard had fallen on the fire. She rushed to him, pulled him from the fire and put out the flames with her hands. Richard was not badly hurt and after only a couple of days in hospital recovered completely. His mother's hands were destroyed. The following day Richard went off to school as usual and at 4 o'clock returned home with two of his friends. His father overheard him as they came through the door. 'Look at my mum's hands,' he said, 'they show how much she loves me.'

If we would know what God is like we must look at Jesus. The distinctive Christian doctrine of God is best summed up in the words of Edward Schillito in his poem 'Jesus of the Scars'.*

The other Gods were strong but thou wast weak.
They rode but thou didst stumble to a throne.
Yet to our wounds only God's wounds can speak
And not a God has wounds but thou alone.
God's wounds show how much he loves me.

---

* Quoted by William Temple in *Readings in St John's Gospel* (Macmillan, 1961), chapter 20.

The 'Way' to God is always Jesus ('I am the Way, the Truth and the Life', John 15), even though we may not be conscious of it. For many Christians the Way to meet Jesus is through Good Friday (atonement), for others it is Easter Day (resurrection), for yet others it is Christmas Day (incarnation). For all, God our Father makes himself known in Jesus Christ through his Holy Spirit (Pentecost). In all these ways God is present in his Spirit through Jesus. He makes himself known to us. The Bible tells us that 'God is Love' (1 John 4:8). He shows how much he loves us in Jesus. Love is always vulnerable and as C.S. Lewis says:

> To love at all is to be vulnerable. Love anything and your heart will certainly be wrung and possibly be broken. If you want to make sure of keeping it intact you must give your heart to no one, not even an animal. Wrap it carefully round with hobbies and luxuries; avoid all entanglements; lock it up safe in the casket or coffin of your selfishness. But in that casket, safe, dark, motionless, airless, it will change. It will not be broken, it will become unbreakable, impenetrable, irredeemable. The alternative to tragedy or at least the risk of tragedy is damnation. The only place outside Heaven where you can be perfectly safe from all the dangers and perturbations of love is Hell.†

How different this is from the sort of God many of us have been brought up to believe in. I grew up believing in a God who reminded me of my grandfather, a strict and unreasonable Victorian disciplinarian, who made rules which were impossible to keep and then punished those who broke them. It took many years for me to realise that this is not the God and Father of our Lord Jesus Christ.

---

† C.S. Lewis, *The Four Loves* (Fontana, 1963), p. 136.

When Bishop Timothy Rees CR died in 1939 there was sung at his funeral requiem for the first time, a hymn of his own composition. It is worth reading carefully.

God is Love: let heaven adore him;
God is Love: let earth rejoice;
Let creation sing before him,
And exalt him with one voice.
He who laid the earth's foundation,
He who spread the heavens above,
He who breathes through all creation,
He is Love, Eternal Love.

God is Love: and he enfoldeth
All the world in one embrace;
With unfailing grasp he holdeth
Every child of every race.
And when human hearts are breaking
Under sorrow's iron rod,
All the sorrow, all the aching
Wrings with pain the heart of God.

God is love: and though with blindness
Sin afflicts the souls of men,
God's eternal loving-kindness
Holds and guides them even then.
Sin and death and hell shall never
O'er us final triumph gain;
God is Love, so Love forever
O'er the universe must reign.

This hymn, although not sung until 1939, was the product of Timothy Rees' experience as a chaplain during the First World War. He describes how he spent days and nights burying young soldiers whom he had come to love and many of whom he had prepared for Confirmation. This experience, along with the experiences of such men as

Studdert Kennedy (Woodbine Willy), formed a theology of God as one who suffers with his creation.

> All the sorrow, all the aching
> Wrings with pain the heart of God.

So God is Love, and Love is vulnerable, and in God there is no un-Christlikeness at all. Christianity therefore uniquely among all the world's religions speaks about the crucified God. This is an obstacle, even a scandal to those of other faiths, yet to those of us who are called to be Christians it is a way of knowing God for it is the way in which he makes himself known. We can only love him because he first loved us and love is not just about vulnerability, it is also about longing.

The lover longs for the beloved, God longs for us. When Jesus says 'I thirst' on the cross, he is expressing a longing which is much more than physical. He is showing the extent of God's longing for us, he longs to 'know' us. Being made in the image of God we are made for love, for vulnerability and for longing. 'O Lord,' said St Augustine, 'you have made us for yourself and our hearts are restless until they rest in you.' Christians believe that our longing for God and his longing for us meet at the cross; they meet us at the manger, they meet us at the empty tomb and the Spirit bears witness to this. But how do I know these things for myself?

PRAYER – THE VITAL KEY

The answer is, as always, simple yet profound. I know in my heart through prayer. Listen to the words of Archbishop Anthony Bloom as he speaks about his own conversion. He had no faith. He belonged to a Russian youth group, and one evening under pressure he went in a surly mood to hear a lecture on Christ and Christianity. The rest must be told in his own words:

> I hurried home in order to check the truth of what the lecturer had been saying. I asked my mother whether she had a book of the gospels because I wanted to know whether the gospel would support the monstrous impression I had derived from this talk. I expected nothing good from my reading, so I counted the chapters of the four gospels to be sure that I read the shortest, not to waste time unnecessarily. And thus it was the gospel according to St. Mark which I began to read. I do not know how to tell you what happened. I will put it quite simply and those of you who have gone through a similar experience will know what come to pass. While I was reading the beginning of St. Mark's gospel, before I reached the third chapter, I was aware of a presence. I saw nothing, I heard nothing. It was no hallucination. It was a simple certainty that the Lord was standing there and that I was in the presence of him whose life I had begun to read with such revulsion and such ill-will.

The same experience which could be related over and over again is described by André Louf in his book *Teach us to Pray*: 'For many, many years I was carrying prayer within my heart, but did not know it at the time. It was like a spring, but one covered with a stone. Then at a certain moment Jesus took the stone away. At that the spring began to flow and has been flowing ever since.' ‡

The God who longs for us makes himself known to us in the depths of our hearts. In fact he already dwells there if only we could realise it but for most of the time we are

---

‡ André Louf, *Teach Us to Pray* (Darton, Longman and Todd, 1991).

too busy, we are not in touch with our own hearts. We are pilgrims in search of our hearts but don't seem to have time for the journey. If you would know God take to heart one simple verse from the Psalms, 'Be still and know that I am God.' It is all that is necessary, so simple and yet so difficult. As soon as we try to be still by getting rid of external noises and distractions we are inundated by the internal noises of our memories and imaginings, our fears and our guilt, and the temptation is to rush back into busyness in order to escape from ourselves and thus from the possibility of knowing God. We must persevere in our longing and receive assurance from a host of witnesses to the worthwhileness of the journey to the heart of knowing God.

(J.N.)

2

The People of God

Preparing to go in to preach at a morning communion service in a local Anglican church, I could hear the hubbub of a lot of people talking as they waited for the service to begin. It was the excited sound of people looking forward to something happening. As we robed, the vicar (who was without a curate for the time being) said that he was finding it difficult being on his own. I know what he meant, but it struck me as a curious irony that he should feel on his own with the sound of all that life bursting through the vestry door. The fact is that we have become used to thinking of the Church as consisting primarily of the clergy, with the laity of only secondary, or subsidiary, importance.

Allowing lay people to emerge from their rather passive role and to consider them as equal partners in ministry is a quantum leap many are unprepared to take. And it isn't necessarily only the clergy who find this difficult. Though some undoubtedly regard lay people as fumbling amateurs when it comes to spiritual matters, many clergy seem genuinely to want to make progress in developing the practice of active lay ministry. In a recent and comprehensive mission audit of parishes in the Blackburn diocese, the overwhelming need recorded by the clergy was for lay training in their parishes. Surprisingly, resistance often comes from another quarter. When lay people do begin to find their feet and start exercising their ministry, they are likely to be considered upstarts by their fellows. 'Who do they think they are?' is the comment sometimes heard.

THE LAY VOCATION

The opening example expresses in rather stark terms a principle which may be experienced in some churches in much milder forms. To be fair, many clergy are trying very hard to acknowledge the vocation of lay people and are seriously seeking means to give it full expression. Similarly, thoughtful lay people are working out their vocation in the world with real vision, demanding that their calling as laity be recognised and affirmed. Nevertheless, latent clericalism lies, like a virus, just under the surface of the skin, waiting to be activated. Quite often we can spot telltale symbols that give the game away. For instance, we train lay people to be lay readers, i.e. to work out their vocation as lay people exercising a particular ministry; but we treat them as pseudo-clergy, both in form of dress and in the manner they are expected to conduct their ministry.

This is a sign that cannot lie. The Church seems to feel comfortable only with patterns of ministry which are modelled on the clergy, aping forms of dress and liturgical mannerisms which are universally recognised as clerical. One of the problems we have, of course, is vocabulary. We speak of 'the clergy' and 'the laity' as though they are separate entities, but obviously they are not. Clergy and laity together comprise the fullness of the Church; they belong together as the *laos*, the people of God. A group I was once working with tried to come up with an alternative title for a clergyperson which did not emphasise the clergy/laity divide. A member of the group, tongue in cheek, suggested the title 'Community Faith Consultant'.

We laughed about this, especially when someone else pointed out that the initials spelled CFC, a substance held to be responsible for destroying the ozone layer. Our conclusion was that we were stuck with the titles of laity and clergy we already possess.

The real issue, of course, is not to do with language and titles, but with doctrine and practice. The Church has never had a clear and unambiguous theology of the laity which has given the laity status as laity. Theological ideas such as 'the apostolate of the laity', 'the priesthood of all believers', and 'every member ministry', are frequently used to give credibility to the idea that laity are important, but it is so often done in a way that makes lay people feel that they are still a subsidiary asset to the Church rather than its essence. The Church needs a theology of the laity which defends their calling and vocation to lay ministry, not as an appendix to the doctrine of the Church, but as an organic, integral insight of the Church's understanding and explanation of itself. We must get to the place where we fully acknowledge that lay ministry is in no way inferior to ordained ministry, that it exists as of right because of the call of God, and that it demands a much higher profile in the theology and practice of the Church. An important symbol in this respect is the amount of money spent on training. The Church of England alone spends many millions a year on the selection and training of its clergy and comparatively little on the training of laity. Most diocesan budgets, similarly, contain a much higher figure for clergy training than for lay training. Not that we should spend less on clergy training, for clearly the Church needs well-trained clergy to fulfil the great demands that are made upon them. But we also need to raise considerably our investment in lay training.

A fundamental issue in developing a theology of the laity is to do with the relationship between the Church and the world. In the most easily remembered text in the whole Bible we are told that God so loved the world that he gave his only Son. The world is both the context and the purpose of the Church's existence. The whole of humankind, not just the Church, is the subject of God's love. The salvation and redemption of the world is his aim. To that extent the Church is provisional, an expression of the love of God for the world. The world is the prior entity, with the Church being sent, as the physical and mystical messenger of God's salvation love. In this way the Church finds identity as the Body of Christ, continuing the mission of love made explicit in the incarnation. This obviously has profound implications for a theology of the laity. If God's mission is to reveal his love for the whole world, and if the Church, in its best understanding of itself, is a function, or a vehicle, of that mission, then the ministry of the laity is crucial. Putting it simply, if the ministry of laity is not used to the full, the Church has no hope of fulfilling its purpose. The Church must create a huge army of committed, well-trained people to do the job. Rather than spending all available energy and resources on the minutiae of internal Church concerns, we must redirect our vision to embrace the world for which Christ died.

The call to discipleship, in which our lay people work out their vocation in the places where they live and work, is critically important. It is here that the Church will rub shoulders with the world, and the opportunities to demonstrate the unqualified love of God will occur. The ministry of the clergy, the services of worship, the oversight of bishops, the diocesan staff and administration, must all be mustered with one overriding aim in view, to equip the laity to be the Church – the visible expression of God's love for the world. It is a symptom of a sick Church to be over-concerned with its own well-being. The Bible teaches, through its dynamic and prophetic revelation of God's plan of salvation, that the concerns, dilemmas, victories and tragedies of the world are basic to the true meaning of the Church. Jesus saw, with vivid clarity, that the world is the theatre of his Father's activity, and therefore rooted his own ministry in the streets, homes, market-places and industry of his day. He prayed, 'Thy will be done *on earth* as it is in heaven', calling ordinary men and women (the laity) to be the channels and instruments by which this would be accomplished. To understand the Church we must begin to see it as an expression of God's love for the world, and its ordinary members as the living presence of Christ bringing healing and reconciliation to the brokenness around them. The ministry and vocation to be laity can therefore never be considered as secondary to that of the clergy, but is of primary importance if the Church is to fulfil its role in the mission of God to the world.

BAPTISM: THE ORDINATION TO MINISTRY

It is clear that the baptism of Jesus at the hand of John the Baptist (a layman) marked the beginning of his ministry on earth. It was his ordination service. This truth, of baptism as the commissioning for ministry, has largely been hidden by the theological conflict and folk-religion controversy that has surrounded its practice. In the modern Church, the significance of baptism has shrivelled by comparison with its meaning and use in the apostolic period. It was intended as a sacramental act dramatising a movement from old to new, from darkness to light. By baptism we are placed into Christ and begin a new life joined to him in love, sharing his aims, his priorities, his mission. In the kind of remarkable paradox frequently seen in the New Testament, baptism is both a separation from the world and, simultaneously, a commissioning service of engagement in the world. Through his baptism

Jesus was seen to have the anointing of God to begin his ministry.

The significance of baptism as an act of separation, but also as an act of commissioning, must be recaptured by the Church. It symbolises ordination to discipleship and makes special every single Christian as a minister of Jesus Christ. To be honest, the Church on the whole does not help in this respect. Baptism is frequently conducted with scant preparation and invested with only marginal significance in the overall life of the Church, whereas the ordination of clergy is given great prominence and dignity. Clearly, one would have to say that the ordination of clergy should not be devalued, but that the ordination of disciples through their baptism be given a much higher profile.

Of course, baptism is the sacramental sign common to both clergy and laity alike. It is a unifying principle, symbolising a common membership of the Church, and commitment to a common mission in the world. It has both a divine and a human aspect, the sacramental form bearing witness to an act of God, and the use of water signifying a bonding to the world. In baptism we are lifted up to God and rooted back into the earth. Every Christian disciple therefore becomes a bridge between God and the world. To turn to Christ, which is the significance of baptism, is to declare our willingness to embrace the principles of discipleship outlined by Jesus. In particular, it puts on record our availability to be sent out in true apostolic faith to be the messengers and witnesses of his redeeming love. Baptism is the ordination or commissioning to ministry for every disciple of Jesus.

THE CALL TO ORDINATION

What, then, is to be the role of the ordained clergy and what function does ordination serve? Bishop John Robinson pinpointed this question in an essay called 'The Ministry and the Laity'. 'What is distinctive', he asked, 'about the ordained ministry?' It can never be good enough to try and define the role of the ordained clergy in terms of their ability to do certain things other people cannot do, i.e. consecrate the elements at communion or pronounce absolution. At best this is simply too negative, at worst it invests clergy with some form of quasi-magical property never intended. John Robinson underlined the truth that the entire Church is a royal priesthood, and every member has a share in that priesthood by virtue of baptism. The clergy are commissioned to exercise, in the name of the Church, the ministry that belongs to all the members. They do not therefore act in a vicarious role as if doing ministry in the place of the laity, but in a representative role as coming alongside them, symbolising the involvement and commitment of the whole Body of Christ. The clergy are given formal authority to preach and proclaim in the name of the whole Church what every member has the right and duty to proclaim. They are given formal authority to exercise the ministry of reconciliation and forgiveness which belongs by right to every member of the Church as a healing community. They are given formal authority to preside at the celebration of the Eucharist which is the celebration of the whole people of God. Bishop Robinson emphasised the fact that every celebration is a lay celebration. The celebrant is the *laos*, of which the bishop or presbyter is 'the president'. The early church never used the term 'the celebrant' of an individual, the Eucharist was always a con-celebration of the whole people of God. In the Orthodox Church it is impossible to have a celebration without lay people present. A celebration which excluded them would be invalid.

Because the clergy occupy a key place in the Church, their calling, selection and training are of the utmost importance. In practice the level of ministry in a local church seldom rises above that of its leaders, and that is why the quality of ordination candidates must always be more important than quantity. The clergy are the ones who are called to model the ministry the whole Church must engage in, and see it as their main business to provide the inspiration, encouragement and training that will enable the laity to fulfil the task of ministry.

TRAINING AND THE GROWTH OF SELF-CONFIDENCE

Theological reflection on the nature of the ordained ministry is crucial. If we insist that the ordained person is exercising a *vicarious* ministry as opposed to a *representative* ministry, then every act of ministry engaged in by lay people will be seen as a threat, diminishing the authority and usefulness of the clergy. This thought casts its shadow over a great deal of the debate on lay ministry, and lies behind a basic mistrust many clergy seem to have of lay involvement. If laity are given more ministry, many clergy fear that their own ministry will be correspondingly restricted. If, however, ordained ministry is seen as truly representative of the whole body this tension disappears; the ministry of clergy and laity expands together.

Hans Rudi Weber, a Swiss theologian, put it like this: 'The laity are not the helpers of the clergy so that the clergy can do their job, but the clergy are helpers of the whole people of God, so that the laity can be the Church.' This makes the leadership and training role of the clergy all the more vital. Lay ministry can no longer be seen in terms of amateurish goodwill gestures to help the clergy because they are overworked, nor the strategy of a Church that needs to keep its doors open but cannot afford to pay clergy. If it is to be developed effectively then the clergy have to become the trainers. The implications of this on the selection and training of clergy are far-reaching. If the role of the clergy is to enable lay people to do the work of ministry, their best endeavours must be given to the task of training. The Church of the future needs clergy who are secure enough, emotionally and spiritually, to allow lay Christians to develop their ministries to the full. This means allowing them to learn by practice, even if mistakes are made; it means giving lay people freedom to grow even when they outstrip the clergy in their effectiveness. Many lay men and women are keen to engage in active Christian ministry but lack experience and self-confidence. The purpose of training is to give self-confidence by doing ministry and therefore increasing experience.

The model of training used by Jesus is the most effective known to humankind. It is copied by philosophers, educationalists, industrialists and craftsmen alike – it must therefore be worthy of serious consideration by the Church. The apprenticeship model of training is simple and effective, developing skills and relationships simultaneously.

Jesus called people to follow him and be his disciples. To be a disciple means, above all, to be a learner. How best do people learn? We undoubtedly learn most effectively by doing. Doing ministry under the careful eye and instruction of a good teacher who has allowed us to watch what he has done, gives us the best opportunity to learn ourselves. This is exactly what Jesus did. As part of the preparation for mission, Jesus sent out the twelve (Luke 9:1–11), and the way he did that gives a very clear insight into his method. First, he called the twelve into a relationship with himself (and of course with one another). He shared his life with them, allowing them to get close to him in order that they would be able to understand what he was about. Relationship building is a key part of discipleship because it provides the best incentive to learn. We all know from our schooldays that we learned the most from those who took the trouble to build the kind of relationship with us which gave us freedom to make mistakes without feeling condemned. In the context of this relationship Jesus let his disciples watch carefully what he did, why and how he did it. He then sent them out in twos to do the things they had seen him do. The disciples subsequently returned to him, reporting how they had fared. Sometimes they spoke with great excitement about the things they had accomplished, but on other occasions they reported failure. As the incident in Luke's gospel reveals, Jesus would often then take the disciples with him to a quiet place, presumably to review progress, and to continue teaching, but also to develop further his friendship with them.

This training method is the best there is and can be used to great effect in the local church. It works most effectively when the clergy take the lead in calling, or inviting, the lay leaders of the church into a relationship in which their vision can be shared. The building up of the relationship, and the subsequent building of confidence, become priorities. In this context, lay leaders can see at first hand how their clergy do the work of ministry. The clergy can then stand alongside the lay leaders while they undertake their own ministry, encouraging, correcting and developing such ministry as the need arises. Lay people can then be sent off to do further ministry on their own (or in twos), and come back together to report on how they have fared. The process continues and develops as those being trained in their turn train others. This is discipleship, the means by which the Church was founded and grew. One could become very excited at the prospect of every PCC meeting being the occasion when everyone came to report on how their ministry was developing. Perhaps we should insist that all Church meetings (local, diocesan and national) have something of this quality about them.

(C.A.)

3

Gifts and Ministries for the People of God

The most frustrating and uncomfortable fact about the Christian faith is that everything is gift. In the epistle to the Ephesians 2:8 we read, 'For it is by grace you have been saved, through faith – and this not from yourselves, it is the gift of God – not by works, so that no-one can boast.' This goes against the grain of our fallen human nature. We like to think and believe that we can and must do something to earn love and especially to earn the love of God. 'If you don't behave, mummy won't love you any more' is the opposite of the way in which God deals with us. It seems natural for us to believe that if we do this or believe that, or behave in this or that way God will love us, and that if we don't, he won't. The fact that God loves the greatest sinner as much as the greatest saint is difficult to swallow. Most of us refuse to accept it deep down, even though we accept it in our heads, and we tend to spend our energies in attempting to earn that which we cannot accept as free. This perversion is known as justification by works; it is not Christian; it is the antithesis of the Gospel. Its fruits are pride for the few and guilt for all.

We must begin by knowing our absolute dependence upon God. Jesus said that without him we can do nothing. He did not say that without him we can do some things but we will perform better with him. He actually used the word 'nothing'. Without him we are nothing and we have nothing.

But that is not all, it is only the beginning. The first and greatest gift which we are given is God himself. There is a psychiatrist in New York who is known for his work with catatonic schizophrenics. His name is Dr John Rosen. Normally doctors remain separate and aloof from their patients, as a sort of defence mechanism against feeling pain when things go badly. Dr Rosen isn't like this though, he moves into the ward with them. He places his bed among their beds. He lives the life they must live. Day to day, he shares it. He loves them. If they don't talk, he doesn't talk either. It is as if he understands what is happening. His being there, being with them, communicates something that they haven't experienced in years – *somebody understands*. But then he does something else. He puts his arms around them and hugs them. He holds these unattractive, unlovable, sometimes incontinent persons, and loves them back into life. Often, the first words they speak are simply, 'Thank you'.

This is what Jesus did for us. He moved into the ward with us. He placed his bed among our beds. Those who were there, those who saw him, touched him and were in turn touched by him and restored to life. The first word they had to say was 'thank you'.

The gifts which God showers upon us are truly staggering. He gives us life and he would love us into fullness of life. Our potential for God is greater than any of us can fully appreciate. The great spiritual writers refer to this as *Capax Dei*, our capacity for God. Yet because we are who we are this treasury of gift is buried deep inside us. For much of the time we cannot believe that it is there, we have too low an estimate of ourselves. God is the only realist; he sees us as we are with all the many debilitating sins and weaknesses which capture us. 'Long my imprisoned spirit lay, fast bound in sin and nature's night,' confessed Charles Wesley. But God also sees that which is hidden: 'man looks at the outward appearance, but the

Lord looks at the heart' (1 Samuel 16:7). God sees the treasury of his grace, his gifts hidden in the depth of our heart. As was said in a previous chapter, life is a journey. 'I am a pilgrim in search of my heart' and there we find not only God himself but also the gifts which God has so generously bestowed upon us. It is indeed the treasure buried in a field, the pearl of great price. The key to the discovery is prayer, that is, allowing God to pray in us or more correctly recognising that God is praying in us all the time, for prayer too is a gift and is already there. The gift is recognised in silence. There is no short cut to 'Be still and know that I am God'. Worship without silence is in grave danger of becoming self-indulgent.

I would like to suggest that there are two kinds of silence, 'inner' and 'outer'. We can do something about outer silence – inner silence is a gift into which we may enter. Outer silence is more than simply an absence of noise though most of us find that difficult enough to cope with. How many of us switch something on when entering a quiet house? We feel uncomfortable with silence and need a television, radio or conversation in the background at least. We run away from outward silence because when there are no external noises, the sounds which are inside our heads begin to get louder, the clamourings which come from our anxiety, our loneliness and our insecurity, and we try to keep these at bay by running away from silence. So when we have removed external sounds we then have to learn how to be attentive and not be distracted by the inside noises. Most of us cannot do this for very long. An hour of quiet time might consist of fifty-five minutes of inward noise and, if we are very fortunate, five minutes of stillness, of silence when we can be attentive. For outward silence is simply a preparation in order that we might be attentive to God. In other words silence is there so that we can prepare ourselves for that gift of the knowledge of the presence of

God which is the heart of contemplation or 'inner' silence. God will give us this gift when he feels that it is appropriate. Our job is to wait in stillness and silence for the gift. God will move the stone which is covering our hearts, but when he thinks fit, which is probably when we least expect it.

Once we realise that all we can do is wait in silence, once we realise our need of God and that everything depends on him, then the door is open and our capacity for God is endless. If we think of gifts as possessions of our own, then their use will be limited to our natural strength. If, however, we realise that gifts are God's, then all we have to do is not get in the way of allowing God to use them. We can let God get on with the ministry to which we are called. There is therefore no essential difference between waiting upon God in prayer and exercising the gifts which God has given us. Both are at heart simply a matter of not getting in the way, of allowing God to be God and work through us. God will draw out the gifts we need to match the tasks he gives us. If the call of God to some particular ministry is discerned in you by others, then respond with fear and trembling lest you are tempted to rely on your own strength. But do not be afraid, for the gifts you need have already been given to you even though no one has seen them yet! I worked for nine years in a parish which was described as a difficult parish because 'there was a marked absence of gifted laity in places like that'. (This was a large overspill council estate.) How inaccurate. Gifts abounded; many were hidden in lives full of pain, but the *Capax Dei* was every bit as much there as anywhere in the world and, from time to time, I was privileged to glimpse this capacity realised in earthy, holy lives. What was so often missing was confidence in God and bringing that out was my job, my privilege and my joy. The priest's role in all this is to help enable it all to happen and, maybe, especially to learn from and to help to point out to his fellow Christians the real magnetic holiness that lives and grows in them. We are bringers of confidence, for holiness would be the last thing which folk would claim for themselves. I don't mean a narrow self-righteous sort of piety but the expression of a deep caring for God and for our fellow men and women, and there are plenty who have been given this gift. A favourite anecdote of mine is about a woman – a good 'Protestant' – who had a girl in her guide company who was dying of cancer at thirteen. The girl was a Roman Catholic and she and her family wanted to make a pilgrimage to the shrine of Our Lady at Lourdes. Now this woman did not really believe in 'that sort of thing' but said that if the girl wanted to go she would go. And so, in two weeks – mostly in pouring rain – she went round every door on the estate and collected £465. If they said, 'We're not Catholic', she said, 'Neither am I, cough up', and they did. During the same fortnight her son was injured by an IRA bomb in Belfast. It made no difference; she collected the money and the girl went to Lourdes. Now this woman has never heard of the word ecumenical – she probably wouldn't be able to pronounce it – but that is the sort of holiness I am here to learn from and to point out.

What so often holds us back is that we rely on our own strengths and hide our own weaknesses because we want to be in control, make plans and possibly do God a favour. In so doing we are doomed to failure.

If we read carefully the story in John 13 of Jesus washing the disciples' feet, we come close to the heart of the matter. It is true that part of the meaning of this passage is to be seen in Jesus setting an example to his disciples who are to do the same as he has done, that is, to serve one another. But the heart of the passage lies, to my mind, in the encounter between Jesus and Simon Peter. When Jesus stoops to wash his feet, Simon Peter refuses. 'You shall never wash my feet,' he says to Jesus. Jesus replies, 'If you do not let me wash your feet you have no part in me.' The heart of discipleship is what we allow Jesus to do for us, not what we do for him.

So you are gifted, and when you were baptised you were certainly called, chosen by God. Those of us who were baptised as infants are particularly conscious of the words of Jesus: 'You did not choose me, but I chose you' (John 15:16). God's patience is infinite; he gifts us and calls us and waits, never coercing us. He waits for us to respond to his call and recognise his gifts. He patiently accompanies us on this often long journey to the heart.

There are three callings: the common, the particular and the unique. The first is, as it implies, common to all of us: to abide in Christ and to know that he abides in us. This vocation includes the call to discipleship, to prayer, to evangelism, to play our part in the common life and worship of the people of God; to witness by deed and word the saving love of God in Jesus Christ and to allow ourselves to be changed, transfigured into his instrument to be used for the bringing into being of his kingdom. This would seem to be enough for any of us, but there is more. The particular vocation is to be found within the common vocation of all. In common parlance it refers to what we call 'vocations' (for example, ordination, nursing or a call to the religious life). Some are called to particular ministries within the people of God. Those so called are not better, more important nor holier than the rest of God's people. On the contrary those who are most effective in particular ministries know that they are 'wounded healers'.

The third calling is the unique vocation. There are no two people alike. Every one of us is unique, there has never been anyone quite like each of us and there never will be. It follows that each and every relationship in our lives is also unique. However close a father may be to his children, although he loves each one of them with all his heart, yet he loves each one differently and each child has the potential to love his or her father in a unique way. If this is true of our human relationships, it is no less true of our relationship with God. The staggering fact is that God loves you in a way in which he can never love anyone else and you have the potential to love him in a way which no other human being can. You are precious, therefore, and of infinite worth. But this relationship, this unique vocation, needs time to grow and mature, which brings us back to prayer and to silence, for we need space to be with God and to listen to him.

The words of Jesus – 'You did not choose me, but I chose you' – apply equally to all three vocations and all three require careful attention and discernment if they are to mature. The common vocation needs to be nurtured by the common life and worship of the Church; it needs to be fed at the 'two tables' of Word and Sacrament. The unique vocation requires, as I have said, silence, but it is also helped by being shared with 'a companion' (literally one with whom we share bread). Many of us have found such a companion or spiritual director of immense help. The particular vocation is Christ's, as are the others, and it has to be discerned and recognised by the Church. It does not belong to the individual; it is not the right of any individual, however holy he or she may be, or however convinced they may be about the validity of their call. In fact, some of the greatest leaders of the Christian Church (it is said literally) were dragged screaming and kicking to their ordination. Among them are St Irenaeus and St Augustine. The emphasis on being chosen by Christ through his Church has been highlighted in recent years in the selection of Local Ordained Ministers. If we believe that the Church is the Body of Christ, and that it is he who chooses us and not we him, then we must take it very seriously when after prayer and thought we are asked to consider our call to any ministry of the Church. We must not refuse the call on the grounds that we are not gifted enough, for we are. God has already seen to that.

(J.N.)

4

Is My Church Worth Joining?

THE PROBLEM OF EXCLUSIVISM

A colleague recently told me a story he had heard about a church that had been known for many decades as 'Highmoor Baptist Church'. (The name is fictitious for the purpose of the story.) In an attempt to move away from the denominational exclusivism implied by this title, the leaders had decided to rename it 'Highmoor Christian Church'. This, it was hoped, would encourage a more open attitude among its members, and break down unnecessary barriers between the church and the wider community. Incensed by this change one stalwart of the church was heard to say, 'I have been a Baptist for almost fifty years, no one is going to start calling me a Christian now.'

Somewhere along the line a principle of exclusivism has crept into the Church. Many members regard the church as their personal property and will resist any kind of change with astonishing tenacity. This clearly creates difficulty when the church is seeking to make important changes in its structure or worship, especially when such changes are considered necessary to make it easier for people to come in from outside. Someone once said that it is about as easy for a non-churchgoer to walk into a church as it is for the average member of the Mothers

Union to walk into a betting shop. The church must look seriously at the barriers it presents to those it claims it wants to reach, otherwise it will become increasingly marginalised and seen to be irrelevant by the vast majority of the population. It takes a great deal of courage and determination to come through the church doors only to find that you have entered a mysterious world with codes of practice which seem designed to be impenetrable. You will probably be handed a book, or perhaps several books, and then walk into the church confronted by a number of people's backs. You slip into a pew wondering if it is all right to sit anywhere. If you sit near the front you feel conspicuous and have to keep turning around to check you aren't still standing when everyone else is kneeling. If you sit near the back you feel out of it because you can't quite make out what is going on at the front. You begin to think that it would be helpful if someone came up to you to explain, but no one does. Just as you are beginning to feel you have made a big mistake and should have stayed in bed, somebody does approach you, but you realise that all they want is your money. He had been hiding a collection plate behind his back. A short while after that everyone starts moving around shaking hands with each other. The person sitting nearest to you grabs hold of your hand and mutters something about peace. Peace is, of course, the last thing you are experiencing and you can hardly wait to get out. It is perfectly understandable why many simply give it up as a bad job. In our heart of hearts we may want people who come into our churches to feel welcome, but first we need to recognise that we have created a climate which makes this very difficult.

WHOSE CHURCH?

All of this raises the question, for whom does the Church exist? Some clergy behave as though the Church belonged to them and become fearful when its members begin to express good ideas about how it should be run. In some churches it is fairly obvious that small, but powerful, groups of people control the church, and they make it clear that they intend to ensure it continues to exist to serve their own interests. We can also still find rural communities where the church is controlled by the landowner in a quasi-feudal system where his word is law.

But whose Church is it? In a proper biblical sense we would have to say it is Christ's Church. He is its head and the source of its life. To say this, however, does not tell the whole story, because human 'ownership' is also involved. The church exists because a community of people, who are the local expression of the wider Church and subject to its authority, have formed and shaped it, and in a very real sense have come to 'own' it. However, this ownership cannot be defined in terms of possession, but rather in terms of stewardship. Stewardship, by its very nature, implies accountability and an exercise of ministry with responsibility and love. That is, the church is cared for by its members in order for them to nurture its life and offer that life as a gift to others. God so loved the *world* that he gave it his Son, he so loves the world that he has given it his Church. The Church is God's gift to the world. It was called into being and nurtured into life as a gift to those outside it. It is a mystery, but the church that does not give away its life loses it altogether. The *ekklesia* is the community of those summoned out of their homes to come and meet with God. It can never be truly understood as an exclusive gathering of like-minded people, but rather as an invitation to *all* to come and meet with

God. To become exclusive and inaccessible to all people is to cease to be the church. In truth, the church belongs to those outside it. The movement from 'possession' to 'stewardship' is therefore one of the most important thresholds for most Christians to cross.

IT'S DIFFICULT TO CHANGE

A legend exists about a great teacher whose cat always followed him to worship. The cat distracted the worshippers, so he ordered that the cat be tied up. The teacher died but his followers continued to tie the cat during evening worship. After the cat died another was brought and tied during worship. Centuries later learned treatises were written by scholarly disciples on the liturgical significance of tying up a cat while worshipping. This is admittedly a caricature; nevertheless, it shows how prone we are to sanctify irrelevancies and to argue for their continued existence against all reason. Traditions develop because things have always been done in a particular way, and we will always find those who will defend that tradition, come what may. It has been said about the Church that it believes in change, as long as it doesn't make any difference. Most Christians would say that they are reasonable human beings and would want to argue that the Church should be there for all people, but still have great difficulty facing the changes necessary for that to happen. So much of our security is bound up in buildings, well-tried structures, and familiar things. There is nothing particularly wrong with that until it prevents us from seeing that we have made our churches a closed shop to all but the very courageous and determined.

Many Christians who seriously face up to the question posed by this chapter answer by saying that their church is worth joining, but they can see why so many people are put off. Stuffy hymns, boring sermons, cold buildings, unfriendly congregations, and inflexible attitudes are among the many reasons given. However, there is a growing feeling that our church communities have to face up to change if they are going to survive. Both growth and decay point firmly to the need for change. If a church is declining, it must consider the reasons for this and begin to develop a strategy for growth. If a church is growing, it will be forced to look at its total life, and begin to adapt, to accommodate those with no background or experience of church life. If the Church truly exists for the sake of those outside it, we have to make it much easier for them to be part of it.

Curiously enough, it isn't usually the liturgies and forms of service that put people off, although they are important factors to consider. It's the lack of a sense of community, of belonging, that most find difficult. Coupled to this, there is a general sense of purposelessness, and of the irrelevancy of the Church to modern life, which keeps many people of goodwill permanently on the fringes. Basically, they cannot see the point of becoming part of a Church which seems to serve no useful purpose.

The Church, perhaps especially the Church of England, must face the fact that it has failed to proclaim the Gospel. The challenge, given by Jesus, of changed lives, and of a community which is simultaneously nurturing, radical and outward-looking, has been watered down or sidestepped altogether. The Church, instead of being fashioned according to the standards given by Christ, has allowed itself to be formed by prevailing secular influences. This has produced a cocktail as unpalatable to thoughtful churchgoers and non-churchgoers alike. Consequently, it offers no real alternative to the many secular views that exist in society today. Thoughtful people see this and wonder what, if anything, is distinctive about the Church.

THE NEED FOR A MISSION AUDIT

As mentioned earlier, the diocese in which the authors are currently working engaged in a parish audit. As much as anything, this was designed to encourage church leaders to think about the priorities of the church in relation to the local community, and to assess how much time, energy and money was being spent on mission as well as on maintenance. Obviously, responses varied from parish to parish but the whole process gave some idea about how user-friendly and outward-looking our church communities are.

There is a legend about an oyster that saw a loose pearl which had fallen into a crevice on the ocean bed. After great effort she managed to retrieve the pearl and place it just beside her on a leaf. She knew that humans valued pearls and thought that if a pearl diver showed up he would see the pearl and leave her alone. One day a diver came; however, his eyes were conditioned to look for oysters and not isolated pearls resting on leaves. He grabbed the oyster which did not happen to have a pearl, and left the pearl to be lost forever. We think we know exactly where to look. That is why we so often fail to see what God is doing.

We are conditioned to see the things we want to see, and consequently do not see things as they really are. We need to listen very carefully to what people outside of the Church say about us. Some of the more enterprising churches in the Blackburn diocese had the courage to seek responses from the wider community, and discovered that the things that preoccupied the church were of no interest to people outside it. In other words, the church was operating to a narrow and fixed agenda without thinking about whether God was actually in it, or reflecting for a moment on the relevance of their activity to the outside world. At a recent meeting someone told the story of a large city-centre church that had completed a major refurbishment of its premises. This had been done apparently without any significant research into local needs. With the building finished the question had to be asked about how it was going to be used. Close to the church there was a large shopping centre. The leaders of the church approached the manager of this centre to try and build a relationship between the church and the people who worked in the stores. The manager, who had never been in the church, said that their immediate need was to have a place to congregate, outside of the stores, in the event of a fire. The leaders of the church were somewhat taken aback thinking of their expensive new carpets, but agreed that the church could become an assembly point. From this, all kinds of contacts developed in which the church could open up its doors to members of staff and exercise a fruitful ministry. The church began by thinking that God was calling them to offer a 'spiritual programme', but he was actually insisting that they began by serving. We are so conditioned to look in one particular direction that we fail to see the obvious coming at us from different directions.

Mission audit means that we try to find out the facts about the present so that we can prepare more effectively for the future. It involves looking outward as well as inward, reflecting on the needs of the local community as well as on those of the church. It means we have to consider ways of devoting more energy and resources to mission, taking seriously the ministry of church members at home and at work as well as in the church. It will undoubtedly involve a consideration of what must be dropped in order to give Christians time and energy to concentrate their efforts outside the church. The hardest thing, of course, is to drop some of the things we are doing in the church so that we can spend time listening to people outside its walls. We need a vision of a church which inspires its members through its preaching and teaching, its sacramental life and worship, its fellowship and love, enabling them to sustain witness through friendship and citizenship in the communities in which they live. The church must rediscover its essential vocation to listen, both to God and to those outside it. In a nutshell this is what mission audit is about.

The Parochial Church Council of a rural church in Lancashire met for a day of prayer and reflection. Their purpose was to try and see the way forward for the church in terms of mission in the village in which they lived. Their conclusion was that they needed to establish a small planning group to do an audit, both of the church and of the community. The obvious person to convene this group was clearly already over-committed. After debating the matter two people on the PCC agreed to take on some of this person's responsibilities in order for her to concentrate on the audit. This was a very important step because it meant that the PCC were taking seriously the process of mission, and at the same time, were attempting to ensure that key personnel were not overloaded.

Audit involves a process of balancing priorities and resources. The church needs to look carefully at its structures, but it also needs to create vision. Overloaded structures will discourage even the most enthusiastic Christians, whereas lack of vision robs them of motivation. Part of the audit is to plant a vision of a church that is able to reach out to the community around it, but also to make sure that the vision is not doomed to failure because of the exhaustion of Christians who have to work flat out to maintain the church's structures. Passing ministry or specific responsibilities on to others, or being prepared to drop altogether some of the church's activities, is an essential part of the mission audit process. If we simply keep loading our church members with more and more tasks we ultimately disable them. One of the key questions in mission audit must be, 'What are the church's priorities?'

Few would doubt that one of the most urgent priorities facing the Church today is that of making itself more accessible, and more welcoming towards those who have no church background.

POSTSCRIPT ON MISSION AUDIT

As Christian leaders involved in the training and encouragement of the whole Church the authors are aware of the vocabulary that is increasingly used when the future of the Church is being considered. Audit, mission statement, empowerment, appraisal and performance-related criteria seem to be the common currency of serious discussions to do with revitalising the Church. As the previous section indicates, these are concepts to be valued, but they are not the only, and certainly must never become the main, criteria by which the Church of God, and the effectiveness of its ministry, are assessed. The Church, which is the Body of the living Christ, has far richer sources of empowerment than seem to be indicated in the avalanche of articles and reports produced about its current condition. Biblical and historical traditions are full of insight and encouragement for those prepared to look. The abiding reality is that the Holy Spirit is prepared to use ordinary people and ordinary things, thereby to accomplish extraordinary acts of grace and love. This mystery is unquantifiable and certainly inaccessible to standard secular procedures of review.

It is curious the way the Church has received, as though they were new, concepts like appraisal and audit. The reality, surely, is that the secular world has adopted important Christian insights, such as *audit* which simply

means 'to listen', *mission statement* which is another name
for 'vision', and *appraisal* which has at its heart the essential Christian virtue of praise. Considerably more curious
is the fact that many Christians are unaware of this process of absorption. It is not unusual to hear Church
leaders, keen to chart what they think is a new way
forward for the Church, using as markers essentially
Christian truths recycled in secular form. However, in the
process they have lost their power as Christian virtues
and have been served up as pale and neutered reflections
of the gifts God originally intended. It sometimes appears
as though the Church is the last to understand and
appreciate the gifts and grace at its disposal. We remain
content to follow limply behind as each new 'progressive'
idea is hailed by secular and commercial concerns, and
then discarded, managing only to catch worn-out
strategies as they are dumped at the tail-end of their shelf-
life.

The fact is that the Church is provocatively on the verge
of renewal. In order for us to go ahead we need prophetic
leadership working in harmony with the Holy Spirit to
call the Church to a life of faith. Of course we can, and
must, use all means at our disposal, including mission
audit, to increase the efficiency of the Church, as long as
we do not lose sight of the power of the Holy Spirit to
revitalise and empower. There is nothing about the
Church to make us pessimistic, other than its inherent
tendency to underestimate the power of God.

WHAT IS A SUCCESSFUL CHURCH?

'As a naturally laid-back denomination the Church of
England has always sought its thrills by frightening itself
to death.' This comment of Gerald Priestland no doubt
applies equally to denominations other than the C. of E.,

but it certainly captures the mood of anxiety frequently experienced by the Church in crisis. It is passing strange that the community which claims to rely on the power of Christ finds it so hard to trust him when things start to go wrong. We are so conditioned to want a successful church that we begin to fall apart when money gets tight or when numbers decline. Success is a god which takes many captives in the Christian Church. A church which can report increased membership and increased giving is deemed to be successful. However, there may be more to it than that. Biblical insight keeps pace to a different rhythm. By worldly standards we could hardly claim that Jesus was successful, but he was incredibly effective. His emphasis was on authenticity and faithfulness, never on achieving success by the world's standards. He attracted people then, and continues to attract people now, precisely because he was different and offered an alternative way of life. As a Church we need to be very clear that our main business is to be the kind of community through which people can always find Christ, which challenges its members to true discipleship, and which offers genuine love to all people.

Perhaps we need to have greater understanding of the pressures people face in their work and home environment. A mature Christian commenting on the tendency of his church to spend too much time arguing over comparatively minor issues said, 'I have to face this every day at work. I'm blowed if I am going to put up with it at church as well.' The thing that was most worrying about this comment was the fact that he was rapidly coming to the conclusion that his church was not worth joining. Obviously, in that frame of mind, he was not going to try very hard to persuade others to join it. A church which offers no real alternative to the organisations and systems which control and depress people in their daily work is not going to survive.

One of the most pervasive and destructive elements in society today is a 'spirit of competition'. No matter where you look, in education, politics, health care and industry, people are being forced to compete. League tables, budgets, policies and attainment targets have become the common currency of competition between schools, universities, hospitals, market economies and political parties. We are passive victims of a force which is out of control. The tragedy is when the Church appears to endorse, and seek to reproduce, this spirit of competition. Competition, of course, has some positive elements. It can encourage excellence in sport and in the achievement of high personal targets. It becomes destructive when people cannot cope with another's success and can only feel good when others fail. It can even go further than this. For instance, in a world-class ice skating competition one contender was physically disabled in order to prevent her winning. You only have to look at the educational system to realise how thoroughly we are all infected by the spirit of competition. Rivalry in getting good grades is rewarded, not only when someone has done well, but also when it becomes clear that others have done badly. Competition engenders an ungenerous attitude which takes delight in another's failure. Observe any discussion group, whether in school, university, workplace or church, and you will see the effects of competition at work. Someone will speak, and rather than listen and learn, others will be concentrating on preparing their own contribution so that they will appear to shine. Putting people down, rather than receiving what they can give, seems to be the object of the exercise. The name of the game ceases to be learning, and becomes a form of competitition in which knowledge and wisdom are no longer gifts to be shared, but missiles to take out another's point of view.

Sadly, one senses this spirit of competition at work in

the Church. Recent painful discussions about the ordination of women have undoubtedly sparked off some
healthy theological debate, but have also unearthed a
decidedly unhealthy cluster of attitudes in some who
have championed opposing points of view. At a parochial
level, the spirit of competition often manifests itself in
power struggles to gain places of influence with the aim
of safeguarding minority interests. Clergy are frequently
made to feel guilty because numbers of confirmations,
baptisms and communicants are declining. Each diocese
has its unofficial league tables which exist in the 'mind' of
the establishment, and which record levels of giving and
statistics of parochial activity, inevitably feeding a spirit of
competition. In all kinds of subtle ways leaders are made
to feel inadequate if their churches are not registering
high scores in the 'shadow' league tables.

A damaging consequence of this is that people feel
devalued. They become self-conscious, insecure and
defensive. Clergy find it hard to confess to others that
things are not going too well in case it shows them up in
a poor light. People find it less easy to share weaknesses
in case someone, at some stage in the future, uses it
against them. The real sadness is that the spirit of competition isolates us. We dare not reveal who we truly are
because of a fear that others will trade on that knowledge
in order to gain some sort of advantage. Competition
breeds isolation. Occasionally, we may find those who,
seeking new meaning for their lives, come into contact
with the Church in the hope that they may find refuge
from the spirit of competition and the sense of isolation
that goes with it. It is a tragedy if the Church simply
mirrors the environment they are trying to leave behind.

It would be foolish to pretend that the Church of the
New Testament was perfect. It manifestly was not. It contained people who were controlled by the spirit of competition. On one occasion, John told Jesus that the disciples

had seen a man driving out demons in his name. They told him to stop because he was not one of their group (Mark 9:38). They were clearly worried about competiti-ton and argued about who was the greatest among them. On another occasion, James and John came to Jesus and asked if he would give to them the places of power and privilege in his coming kingdom. The other disciples were furious when they found out, not because they didn't think these positions were important, but because James and John had tried to get there first, establishing priority for themselves. Jesus' response to this was to teach them all about servanthood. 'Whoever wants to become great among you must be your servant, and who-ever wants to be first must be slave of all' (Mark 10:43–4). This verse contains the secret of Jesus' life and ministry, and suggests the way forward for us. If, instead of being dominated by the need to compete, we were able to serve each other, we would create an environment in which people would be built up and encouraged rather than undermined. The great movement of the Holy Spirit is to plant within us a spirit of servanthood and encourage-ment, instead of a spirit of competition. Imagine the effect this could have on people as they entered our churches to find a community that existed to serve them. The creation of community, as a place of fellowship and affirmation, where people are loved for who they are, and where the overriding motive is servanthood, would be immensely attractive. Servanthood is the practical means whereby the Spirit of God moves us from competition to encour-agement, and from isolation to community.

Is your church worth joining? It could be.

(C.A.)

5

The Holy Spirit

The Holy Spirit is frequently represented in the Bible by using natural substances as symbols, such as water, oil, wind and fire. This, it seems to me, offers plenty of food for thought as we seek to understand who the Holy Spirit is, and what he does. The Scriptures and Christian tradition portray the Spirit as a mysterious and indefinable presence who acts sometimes with frightening power, and at other times with very great gentleness and sensitivity. The use of symbols in the Bible helps us to enter into the mystery, and gives us some understanding of the part the Holy Spirit plays in giving life, meaning and direction to the human spirit.

THE SYMBOL OF BREATH

The Hebrew word for spirit, *ruach*, and the Greek word, *pneuma*, are both also used to convey the idea of wind or breath. The Spirit of God is a renewing breath, filling and energising humankind. He is mysterious, powerful, like a mighty wind that cannot be domesticated. The twin ideas of life-giving breath and powerful storm are woven together in both Old and New Testaments when they seek to describe the action of the Holy Spirit. The breath of God can be gentle, raising us to new life. The wind of God can be boisterous, powerful, sweeping into our lives with invincible force.

For instance, in the startling vision given to the prophet Ezekiel in which he was commanded to prophesy to the valley of dry bones a remarkable transformation occurred. The bones that littered the floor of the valley came together, tendons and flesh appeared on them, and they were covered in skin; but there was no breath in them, and therefore no life. As Ezekiel prophesied, the breath of God entered them; they stood on their feet, a vast army. It is the Spirit of God, his breath, that gives life, transforming an inert carcass into a living being. Although the image is less forceful, the same idea is portrayed at the end of John's gospel when Jesus, in one of the post-resurrection appearances, breathed on the disciples and said, 'Receive the Holy Spirit.' The purpose was to empower, to give new life.

The breath, or wind, of God is mysterious and powerful, hurtling through the fields, withering the grass and causing the flowers to fall, scattering debris and uprooting trees. Jesus uses this imagery, found in Isaiah, to explain the working of the Holy Spirit: 'The wind blows wherever it pleases. You hear its sound, but you cannot tell where it comes from or where it is going. So it is with everyone born of the Spirit' (John 3:8).

The symbol of breath and wind gives us the imagery of both gentleness and power. The Spirit of God is like a refreshing life-giving breath without which human beings are deflated, spiritually inert. The Spirit of God is also like a powerful storm that cannot be controlled. All move and bend before him.

He sweeps away the debris and clutter that has been accumulating over the years and which simply gets in our way, tripping us up when we try and follow after the Lord. He shakes the very foundations of the Church, removing the dead wood of fruitless human traditions so that new growth can emerge. It's not difficult to see, therefore, that to be open to the Holy Spirit requires courage.

THE SYMBOL OF FIRE

Storm and fire are two of nature's most devastating agents, yet they exist as biblical symbols of God the Holy Spirit. It is important that we find out why. As well as the more obvious uses of fire which may have spiritual significance, for instance when it is used for cooking, to give warmth or to refine the impurities out of precious metals, the Old Testament especially invests it with particular meaning as an indicator of the presence and power of God. It is used negatively to destroy idols, and it is used positively as an instrument of Temple worship to offer sacrifice and burn incense. Furthermore, the symbol of fire indicates the presence of God in particular manifestations.

The angel of the Lord appeared to Moses from within a burning bush on Mount Horeb, commissioning him to lead the people of Israel out of Egypt (Exodus 3:1–6). In this incident fire was used as a symbol of the holy presence of Yahweh. By it Moses was persuaded of the trustworthiness and power of God, and committed himself to fulfil the mission he was called to. In this connection two other Old Testament stories spring to mind: Elijah's confrontation with the prophets of Baal on Mount Carmel (1 Kings 18:16–38), and Isaiah's life-changing meeting with God in the Temple (Isaiah 6:1–8).

In order to establish the identity of the one true God Elijah challenged the 850 prophets of Baal and Asherah to a contest. Two altars were to be prepared on Mount Carmel complete with bulls for sacrifice. The prophets of Baal were to call on the name of their god and Elijah would call on the name of the Lord. The one who answered by fire, consuming the sacrifice, was to be acknowledged as the true God. The story unfolds with all the vivid pathos and humour of a comic opera. The prophets of Baal prepared their sacrifice and from morning till evening, shouted and raved and beat themselves into a frenzy, but nothing happened. Elijah mocked and taunted them, making rude comments about Baal, and still nothing happened. Then Elijah called all the people to him and repaired the altar of the Lord. After preparing the wood and the sacrifice he asked the people to drench altar, wood and sacrifice thoroughly with water.

At the time of sacrifice Elijah stepped forward and prayed that the Lord would set fire to the sacrifice, virtually challenging him to prove himself. Then the fire of the Lord fell, burning up the sacrifice and demonstrating for all to see that he is the one true God. In this very powerful drama God revealed his presence in the fire.

The cliff-hanging excitement of this incident could be contrasted with the healing gentleness which marks the use of the symbol of fire in Isaiah's vision. The prophet, having confessed to God that he had unclean lips, clearly made himself vulnerable. A prophet's mouth is his ministry, and ultimately his livelihood. To have unclean lips would disqualify him from ministry as a prophet, and render him useless as the voice of God. However, upon his confession, a seraph (a kind of angel attending the throne of God) flew to him with a burning coal from the altar and touched his mouth. 'See, this has touched your lips; your guilt is taken away and your sin atoned for' (Isaiah 6:7). When God subsequently issued the invitation, 'Whom shall I send? And who will go for us?' Isaiah was able to respond, 'Here am I. Send me!' His response revealed his confidence that God had truly forgiven and cleansed him. He was able to use his voice to demonstrate that he had received forgiveness and healing. In this vision God is seen to be present, acting through the symbol of burning coal to restore Isaiah and qualify him for ministry.

These selected Old Testament accounts of God's dealings with his people serve as a fruitful background to New Testament teaching on the Holy Spirit. From this, understanding begins to emerge about what John the Baptist meant when he prophesied the advent of Jesus, 'He will baptise you with the Holy Spirit and with fire' (Matthew 3:11). Because the symbol of fire is evocative of particular activities and characteristics of God, it is perfectly natural to assume that the visible presence of tongues of fire on the day of Pentecost contained some very clear messages. It specifically spoke of the presence of God in ordinary daily life. God has come among us to reveal his love, to call us to ministry, to empower, to lead and to guide, to heal, to cleanse and to restore. As Moses was called to a particular task, so are we. As Isaiah was commissioned for ministry and enabled by being cleansed and restored, so are we. As Elijah was empowered to challenge godlessness and overcome unbelief, so are we. The fire of the Lord has fallen upon the whole people of God to empower each one, without exception, for service. Fire is an inclusive symbol, it touches all without discrimination. God takes us all seriously as co-workers. In calling us to discipleship he sets in motion a process in which each human contribution makes a difference.

THE SYMBOL OF WATER

For all kinds of obvious reasons water is important. It is especially important in those parts of the world where it is in short supply, so naturally it features significantly in the lives of the people of the Bible. It is equally a problem when there is too much as in the flood, or when there is too little as in the frequent times of drought. Major crises also occurred when water supplies became polluted and undrinkable.

In a bold and remarkable statement, Jesus invited those who were thirsty to come to him and drink. He drew a parallel between the experience of an acute physical thirst which must be satisfied, and the deep spiritual longings which mark every human life. Such longings must find a source of satisfaction, hence the urgent, insatiable, and frequently disappointing search undertaken by many people who frantically invest their hope in possessions, career, or endless sequences of new experiences and relationships. An echo of this fruitless waste is found in the words of Isaiah:

'Come, all you who are thirsty,
    come to the waters;
and you who have no money,
    come, buy and eat!
Come, buy wine and milk
    without money and without cost.
Why spend money on what is not bread,
    and your labour on what does not satisfy?' (55:1–2)

Similarly, Jesus, when talking to the woman of Samaria at the well of Sychar, warned her about the addictive incompleteness of all human experiences compared to the utter fulfilment of eternal life.

'Everyone who drinks this water will be thirsty again, but whoever drinks the water I give him will never thirst. Indeed, the water I give him will become in him a spring of water welling up to eternal life.' (John 4:13–14)

Taking this a stage further Jesus specifically links the symbol of water with the Holy Spirit.

'If anyone is thirsty, let him come to me and drink. Whoever believes in me, as the Scripture has said, streams of living water will flow from within him.'

By this he meant the Spirit. (John 7:37–9)

Those who come to faith in Jesus will not only find spiritual renewal and refreshment for themselves, but will also be a means of refreshing others. Streams of living water will flow out of their innermost being, irrigating the parched human soil around them. This thought is rich in symbolism, evoking many of God's promises given in the Old Testament to create streams in the desert. The exciting reality behind this is simply that the believer will be used as a channel of the Holy Spirit making fertile what was previously barren. The implications of this are enormous, underscoring the New Testament understanding about the apostolic nature of the Church – that is, of a community vibrant with life-giving qualities, constantly moving forward and outward, bringing, like streams in the desert, new life to all in its path.

God has planted in the Church, and in each member of it, a spiritual nature which, when allowed to, will reproduce life. We are to be channels, not repositories, of the Holy Spirit. The nature of the Spirit is to flow, our responsibility is to allow that to happen. We are filled in order to be emptied. Christians, or churches, who try to contain the life of the Holy Spirit, will stagnate like a pool which has neither inlet nor outlet. An encouraging aspect of this symbolism is implicit in the natural properties of the stream itself, which flows without being pushed or forced. Our responsibility is to keep the channel free from obstructions. The hardest lesson many of us have to learn is to stand clear so that we don't become the obstacle.

THE SYMBOL OF OIL

Biblically, oil has both practical and sacramental significance. It was used in the preparation of food, as a basic medicine, and as fuel for household lamps. Such rather mundane practicalities offer insight into deeper spiritual meanings. Food for life, medicine for healing, and oil for light: each contains a rich symbolism which finds an echo right at the heart of the Gospel. In addition, of course, oil was used sacramentally to anoint kings and priests, both as a sign of God's favour and also as a commissioning for service. In this context it came to symbolise the Holy Spirit. When, for instance, the prophet Samuel consecrated David as king he anointed him with oil, 'and from that day on the Spirit of the Lord came on David with power' (1 Samuel 16:13). This connection between anointing and the Holy Spirit is continued in the New Testament. Peter's preaching of the Gospel at the house of Cornelius contained an explanation of the authority and identity of Jesus, 'how God anointed Jesus of Nazareth with the Holy Spirit and power, and how he went around doing good and healing all who were under the power of the devil, because God was with him' (Acts 10:38).

Two facets of this symbolism are well worth exploring, the use of oil as representing the Holy Spirit in healing, and in anointing for ministry. The classic New Testament text to do with healing is contained in the letter of James: 'Is any one of you sick? He should call the elders of the church to pray over him and anoint him with oil in the name of the Lord. And the prayer offered in faith will make the sick person well; the Lord will raise him up' (James 5:14–15). Oil as a symbol of the Holy Spirit points to the ministry of healing given to the Church. This, in turn, indicates the desire of God to bring people to wholeness. Increasing numbers of churches are discovering the power of this symbol and have begun to use the anointing of oil as a sacrament of healing. Oil, of course, has its own healing properties. In that well-known parable of the Good Samaritan, the compassionate traveller used oil to soothe the wounds of the injured man. It is entirely appropriate, therefore, that oil be seen as a symbol of the healing work of God the Holy Spirit. Another interesting aspect of this is revealed in Psalm 133 which sees the anointing with oil as a symbol of unity: 'How good and pleasant it is when brothers live together in unity! It is like precious oil poured on the head . . .' (vv. 1–2). The healing of community is therefore another vital aspect of the Holy Spirit's work. Bringing communities together in understanding, forgiveness and love is a particular emphasis of the Holy Spirit, of which the Church is intended to be a model and sacrament. The healing of families, marriages, and relationships of all kinds is similarly high on the day-to-day agenda of the Holy Spirit. To use an allegory, it is relevant to notice that in the modern world, a major use of oil is to reduce friction. The grace of reconciliation, of bringing people together in love, of experiencing the healing of forgiveness, is implicitly part of the flowing-out of the Spirit of God.

The other biblical use of oil is to do with commissioning for service. Anointing priests and kings as they began their period of office was common in the Old Testament, symbolising the presence and gifting of the Spirit of the Lord to equip for a new task. This is intended as a token of the overwhelming generosity of God that always accompanies the call to love and serve him. 'You anoint my head with oil; my cup overflows. Surely goodness and love will follow me all the days of my life' (Psalm 23:5–6). Anointing with oil is a sign that God is not mean in the distribution of his blessings and his love. Whatever he calls us to do he more than adequately equips us to fulfil. This is supremely evident in the anointing given to Jesus, and is also clear in the anointing given to the disciples. When the apostle John wrote to the churches of the Asian province he reminded them of the anointing (*chrisma*) they had received from Christ which would not be taken away, 'But you have an anointing from the Holy One . . . the anointing you received from him remains in you' (1 John 2:20 and 27).

The anointing with oil for ministry and service is a powerful and moving symbol containing the twin ideas of the Holy Spirit's presence and the generous outpouring of his gifts. Happily, the use of oil is being rediscovered as a relevant and effective sacrament in different contexts. In some cases Confirmation candidates are anointed to signify the beginning of a new phase in their spiritual journey. This carries with it the expectation that there will be an increasing involvement in ministry as disciples of Jesus Christ. Some dioceses are experimenting with the use of anointing at the installation of a new bishop. It has been my practice for some time now when leading a retreat to anoint the retreatants with oil as a symbol, not only of healing, but also of commissioning for a new phase of ministry. It is encouraging that greater imaginative use is being made of this important biblical symbol as the Church seeks to equip increasing numbers for Christian discipleship.

Depicting a fascinating reversal of roles, an incident occurs in the gospels where anointing symbolised both healing and the beginning of new life; not for the person anointed, but for the one doing the anointing. A woman, described rather coyly by Luke as a sinner, came to Jesus with a jar of expensive oil. She wet his feet with her tears, dried them with her hair, and then anointed them with perfumed oil. In this beautiful gesture, which evoked the memory, habits and skills of an entirely different kind of life, she offered the devotion of her new life to her Lord and Saviour.

THE PURPOSE OF SYMBOLS

A symbol is a sign or token, a representative object or substance which serves as a guarantee of that which it symbolises. Christians have used symbols as a focus for contemplation to enable the reality represented by the symbol to take root in the heart. Put simply, reflection on symbols enables particular truths to make the hazardous journey from the mind to the heart. Symbolism helps to convert information into experience. Doctrine may be the Church's formal way of expressing relationship with God, but symbolism can help to make it real. It is a means of bringing belief right into the centre of life, both for the individual and also for the community. We use symbols because they help us to enter into communion with God.

The symbols of the Holy Spirit outlined in this chapter provide an incredibly fertile focus for contemplation. To think of the Spirit of God as breath and wind, as water, fire, or oil enables us to enter more deeply into an experience of the realities they represent. Our understanding is expanded, our experience enriched, and our relationship with God clothed with reality. God becomes accessible.

(C.A.)

6

The Church as a Function of God's Mission

I have never been fortunate enough to be invited to one of those extravagant high society parties where champagne flows like water. I have, however, seen them on film and television. I remember seeing one such party where a huge pyramid of champagne glasses was set up on a table and champagne was poured into the top glass until it overflowed, first to one glass and then to another until the whole pyramid was a cascade of overflowing champagne. The glasses simply waited, empty and expectant, until they were filled and then overflowed. This is one simple way of understanding what mission is about. The late Gonville Ffrench Beytagh, formerly Dean of Johannesburg, once preached a sermon in which he described the Holy Spirit not as proceeding from the Father but as cascading, and I think he had a point.

Mission starts with God. God is 'pure unbounded love' and the love of God and the life of God cascade into our hearts. Mission is the overflowing of this love. It is not something we initiate; it is not something we do; it is not a programme of evangelistic activity to be set alongside all the other hyperactive busyness of Church life; it is our life-blood. We receive, and what we receive overflows. The Church flows from the mission of God.

This principle of receiving and overflowing applies to every aspect of our lives both for good and for ill. I receive love but I also receive hurt from each and every relation-

ship in my life, and both overflow into my relationship
with other people. It follows that the Church, corporately
and individually, needs to be cleansed, purged, purified,
forgiven and healed. In other words, it needs to be made
ready to receive and to be filled to overflowing. This is not
a once-for-all necessity but is a continual process, for, to
extend the metaphor, we get silted up as does a river bed
or an artery and we regularly need to be cleansed. This is
why at the beginning of each Eucharist, before we can be
filled, we ask our Father to 'cleanse the thoughts of our
hearts by the inspiration of your Holy Spirit', and go on to
make our confession both corporately and individually
to God and to one another. We do this in order that
nothing may get in the way of our being filled to overflowing.

Mission is, therefore, not something which we do from
time to time for God. It is God's activity in which he uses
us all the time if only we would not get in the way. The
whole life of the Church can and should be seen as God's
mission. Let us now look at some aspects of the life of the
Church and try to see them for what they really are, part
of God's mission.

WORSHIP

Worship is God's activity. In one of the rites of the Orthodox Church, the Eucharist proper begins when the
deacon announces to the priest, 'It is time for the Lord to
act'. We come with empty hands for him to fill. We offer
ourselves in the best way we know how, but it is the Lord
who acts and his love overflows through worship. In
worship we are put in touch with the living God, yet how
often we see it debased into an occasion for entertaining
the congregation or even God.

It is difficult to put into words the change which occurs

when the local church realises that worship is the activity of God. Those of us who are called to lead worship in many different local congregations experience it in the way in which one sometimes feels carried along by the worship while, in other places, one feels that one has got to carry the worship. The difference is the realisation, or not, that worship is God's activity. It matters little whether the rite is 1662 or ASB or more informal and open-ended worship. The Church of England rejoices in a rich variety of styles which is altogether good. Churchmanship is equally varied but worship comes alive not when the externals are altered one way or another but when we realise that it is not our activity but God's.

FELLOWSHIP

The fellowship of the church is God's activity. The loving presence of the Holy Spirit changing the lives of those who are committed to each other in mutual love is part of God's mission. 'See how these Christians love one another'; 'By this shall all men know that you are my disciples, if you love one another'. People are drawn and held by the quality and the fellowship of the church, but this is something which cannot be artificially created by us, it is God's gift, it is 'the fellowship of the Holy Spirit'. It is not easy for many people to step over the threshold of the church; they feel that they are entering a foreign land and are often extremely self-conscious in doing so. It takes courage to enter into the unknown alone but fellowship can give us that courage. To go with a friend, to sit with a friend is far easier than doing it alone. And for those for whom it is far too big a step to walk into a church, there is the social fellowship of the church which can become the half-way house for those outside where they will notice that Christians can be, in the best sense, more human than others and not less so. This itself becomes magnetic. All this is gift; if it is not recognised as such the fellowship of the church can become the slippery slope towards the church becoming a social club rather than the living Body of Christ.

TEACHING

The teaching of the church is God's activity. He stimulates our minds and opens our hearts to understand in order that we might be enabled to teach others the truth as found in Jesus Christ. The evangelisation of the mind is also part of mission. We must learn not to live in compartments where our minds think one thing and our emotions and our faith teach another. We must argue, discuss and learn to realise that the Christian faith is not unreasonable. We should never be afraid to ask searching questions, never be afraid to say 'I don't know'. We must never be afraid of doubts for God can and does work through our uncertainties. As Baron von Hugel says in the introduction to his *Letters to a Niece*,

> Never get things too clear. Religion can't be clear. In this mixed up life there is always an element of unclearness ... If I could understand religion as I understand that two and two make four, it would not be worth understanding. Religion can't be clear if it is worth having. To me if I can see things through, I get uneasy – I feel it's a fake. I know I have left something out, I have made some mistake.

So long as we do not fall into the trap of believing that God needs protecting by our certainties then all our exploration can be used by him as part of his mission of love. We must learn that teaching and learning are God's activity, and respect and listen to those who are given gifts of great learning.

SERVICE

Service within the community is God's activity of mission, it is an overflowing of his love through his Church. We do not have to label the love and service of our fellow human beings as Christian 'service' by setting up our own agencies to duplicate secular agencies of service. If we do not get in the way, God's love will overflow even if his name is not mentioned and eventually his presence will be recognised. The hidden Christ is present in a thousand and one different places. It is important for us to realise that part of mission is simply recognising the Christ who is already there. The Church does not have a monopoly on God. There is nowhere where Christ is not, that is the glory of our belief; that he descended into hell, rose from the dead and ascended into heaven. We simply have to recognise him, point him out to others and rejoice in his presence. In mission we are not taking Christ anywhere for the love of God overflows into the world as well as the Church. The essential difference between the Church and the world is that the Church is given to recognising whereas the world often does not. Yet he is there in the faces of the poor, the homeless, the starving and also, but more difficult to discern, in the faces of the rich, the careless and the abusers of others. Mother Teresa of Calcutta has something to say about this. Each day she meets Jesus; first at mass where she derives sustenance and strength; then in each needy, suffering soul she sees and tends. They are one and the same: Jesus at the altar and in the streets, neither exists without the other. Our eyes need to be opened to this truth, for we Christians are all too often blind. We do not recognise the Jesus who is already there. In other words we need to be constantly reminded that God's mission is not just through the Church to the world, but also to the Church. None of us has arrived; for each of us the process of conversion and sanctification takes at least a lifetime, so mission is to us and through us. Just as the champagne glass in the pyramid is continually in need of replenishment as it overflows, so it is with us.

(J.N.)

7

Telling Your Story

We all have a story to tell, our own story, unique to each of us. It is a story which is important because it is unique. It is precious to us, to God and, if we are fortunate, to those who love us.

Life without knowledge of its own story is a sad affair because without my story I do not know where I come from and therefore who I am. It is the present-day tragedy of those who suffer from Alzheimer's disease. The loss of memory, of story, is for them the loss of identity. Story is, therefore, an essential ingredient of life.

What is true of the individual is also true of the family, the tribe and the nation. Without a sense of history we lose our identity. Time was when this was taken for granted, when we knew that our past was important and, even though psychology has taught us how vital being in touch with one's story is for the health of the individual, we seem to have lost the art of either telling or listening to stories. We could, therefore, be in danger of losing our memory and our identity too. This is easily accounted for. We tend to become less efficient in the use of those things we do not need or use. Once we learn to read and write, once the printed word replaces the written word, once we can 'look something up' in a memory bank, we no longer need to remember. Even in our century the art of memorising (poems and prayers as well as stories) has declined in our society. The sad result is that in the age of a communications' revolution we seem to be less able or willing to communicate with each other. The art of conversation round a table, over a meal, has been replaced by a silent meal round a television, and we are all the poorer for that. There can be no doubt that for the sake of ourselves and of the society in which we live we need to rediscover how to listen and how to tell our stories.

As Christians we have inherited the greatest story ever told. It goes back to a nation steeped in story-telling – Israel. The stories of Abraham, the father of the nation, Moses, the lawgiver, and David, God's anointed king, are part of our story. Stories of journeys from captivity to freedom, and vice versa, are part of our journey. Stories of promises and broken promises in the context of God's faithfulness are the stories of our promises too. How do we know about these things? We know because from generation to generation these stories have been told until in the fullness of time came the greatest story ever told – that of the birth, life, death and resurrection of Jesus Christ our Lord. The story of our faith is the story of how these stories – God's story – and our stories both individual and corporate meet. When my story and God's meet, what a story there is to tell! But any story, even God's, needs both tellers and listeners.

Unfortunately, as has been implied, most people are not practised at either telling or listening to stories. Our concentration span, so we are told, has shortened dramatically this century. Less than a hundred years ago congregations were used to listening to hour-long sermons but now in some churches there would be complaints were the sermon to last for more than ten minutes. Even TV programmes need a commercial break to enable people to cope with their length. Yet never has the need for more listeners been greater. It is the simplest and deepest way of showing that we care. Many, many people have no one to listen to their story, their joys and their sorrows. So many people need for example simply to share their pain, but how can this longing be met if no one will share with them that most precious commodity of time? Numerous books have been written about the art of listening; it is not the purpose of this chapter to dwell on it save to say that a story without a listener dies and listening is at heart the costly art of giving time and love. Many have been brought to faith simply by being listened to by a Christian. It requires of the listener the gift of patience. Listening is also an integral part of telling stories for, as you become aware of the other person's story, you may discover that your way of presenting God's story and your own is quite inappropriate. Telling stories (how much that phrase has been devalued!) involves patience to listen, the knowledge of one's own story, the knowledge of God's story, confidence to tell and practice in telling.

We do need to know God's story, to soak in the Scriptures and listen to the stories of those who have known God best. They may know what, as yet, we may only know about, but we needn't worry about that for now. We must admit that we do not know, never pretend, share what we can and leave the rest to God.

Have you ever told your faith's story (i.e. how your story and God's story meet)? For many of us our faith is such a private affair that we would never dream of speaking of it (even to those who are near and dear to us). Indeed we prefer to appoint and pay professionals (clergy) to do it for us rather than do it ourselves, but we cannot avoid the fact that it is the responsibility of all the baptised to share the good news of the Gospel. Of course, if we believe the good news for ourselves we cannot resist the longing to share it. It is a joy not a duty, but even if it is something of a duty at first, the telling of a story can itself turn it into a joy for God is in the story and makes himself known through the story.

They say that practice makes perfect and, although this may not be quite true this side of heaven, it does help. Practise your story; it does bring confidence. Practise with a friend who will encourage you and will laugh with you when you make a terrible mess of it.

One final boost to your confidence in the form of a story! On a parish mission a student was asked to speak to a school assembly of almost two thousand eleven to eighteen year olds. He was petrified and begged his tutor to relieve him of the burden of this responsibility. He claimed that he would have nothing to say, he claimed that he would be an embarrassment to himself and every-one around him, he claimed that he would make an awful mess of the occasion. His tutor, however, refused to give in and the student was proved right. He did make a awful mess of the occasion. He stammered and stuttered and could not find the right words, he was an embarrassment to himself and to every one around and yet, at the mission service that evening in the parish church, a group of teenagers arrived who had not been before. When asked what prompted them to come to the service they pointed to the student concerned. 'He did,' they said, and then went on to explain that they knew what it was like to feel foolish and embarrassed in front of others, to feel self-conscious before their peers. They concluded that if some-one believed in something sufficiently to make such a fool of himself there must be something in it and so they had come to find out. The tutor commented that the student could have made a much better job of the assembly but it would never have borne such fruit.

In the telling of stories our weaknesses often speak more eloquently than our strengths.

(J.N.)

8

The Eucharist and Evangelism

Dom Gregory Dix, in his book *The Shape of the Liturgy*, wrote the following words about the command of our Lord to 'Do this in remembrance of me':

> Was ever another command so obeyed? For century after century, spreading slowly to every continent and country among every race on earth, this action has been done, in every conceivable human circumstance, for every conceivable human need from infancy and before it to extreme old age and after it, from the pinnacles of earthly greatness to the refuge of fugitives in the caves and dens of the earth. Men have found no better thing than this to do for kings at their crowning and for criminals going to the scaffold; for armies in triumph or for a bride and bridegroom in a little country church; for the proclamation of a dogma or for a good crop of wheat; for the wisdom of the Parliament of a mighty nation or for a sick old woman afraid to die; for a schoolboy sitting an examination or for Columbus setting out to discover America; for the famine of whole provinces or for the soul of a dead lover; in thankfulness because my father did not die of pneumonia; for a village headman much tempted to return to fetich because the yams had failed; because the Turk was at the gates of Vienna; for the repentance of Margaret; for the settlement of a strike; for a son for a barren

woman; for Captain so-and-so, wounded and prisoner of war; while the lions roared in the nearby amphitheatre; on the beach at Dunkirk; while the hiss of scythes in the thick June grass came faintly through the windows of the church; tremulously, by an old monk on the fifteenth anniversary of his vows; furtively, by an exiled bishop who had hewn timber all day in a prison camp near Murmansk; gorgeously, for the canonisation of S. Joan of Arc – one could fill many pages with the reasons why men have done this, and not tell a hundredth part of them. And best of all, week by week and month by month, on a hundred thousand successive Sundays, faithfully, unfailingly, across all the parishes of Christendom, the pastors have done this just to make the *plebs sancta Dei* – the holy common people of God.*

We 'do this' because it is the Lord's command, anything else seems second-best. And as we do it, over the years the riches of its meaning grow broader and deeper.

A friend of a friend died from an AIDS related illness. He was a practising Christian and had asked that his funeral should take place in one of the leading Anglo-Catholic churches in London where he himself had been baptised a few years earlier. The service took the form of a Requiem Eucharist set, in Latin, to music by Byrd. There were hundreds of candles, clouds of incense, beautiful vestments. In human terms the liturgy was inaccessible to the uninitiated. The church was packed with young and old, most of whom clearly were not used to being in church at all. For many it may well have been their first visit. Yet as the Eucharist went on I could not help noticing

---

* Dom Gregory Dix, *The Shape of the Liturgy* (A. & C. Black, 1945).

how the uninitiated were being caught up in this supreme act of worship. 'Therefore with angels and archangels and with all the company of heavens . . .' As the words were sung windows were opened and I was reminded of Wesley's description of the Eucharist as a 'converting ordinance'.

One of the best books to be published in recent years about the Eucharist is *Lively Sacrifice* by Michael Perham. In it he is at pains to point out that:

> The truth is that the deep purpose of worship is not to evangelise, nor to teach, nor to engender fellowship, but to be in touch with the living God . . . to remind us every time we come, that we do not create worship; we simply join ourselves for a while to the perpetual worship around the throne of God.

And yet the final words in the book are about the Eucharist as evangelism.

> The Church does not set out to evangelise through worship. It sets out to worship but if its worship is authentic, then it will convert. Be it through the simple communion of a house group, or through the Schubert Mass and the clouds of smoke of a solemn Eucharist in a great cathedral, or through the ordinary weekly or daily celebration in any parish church across the land, if the reality of the relationship between God and the worshippers is almost tangible, if it is indeed a lively sacrifice, it will convert.†

This is, in fact, bound to be the case for 'For whenever you eat this bread and drink this cup, you proclaim the Lord's death until he comes' (1 Corinthians 11:26). The

---

† Michael Perham, *Lively Sacrifice* (SPCK, 1992).

celebration of the Eucharist is the preaching par excellence of Christ crucified.

The current fashion in worship is to make it as accessible as possible, to centre worship on ourselves rather than on God, but it is the centring of worship on God which preaches the Gospel and converts the worshipper. From beginning to end the Eucharist is God-centred. Throughout the service everything is addressed to the Father through the Son in the Holy Spirit. I believe that Christianity is caught simply by being with people whose worship is God-centred and there is no more God-centred worship than the Eucharist. It is something like learning to pray. I learnt to pray by being with others as they prayed. There were no lessons, no books, not even any words. I simply knelt in silence in a tiny chapel with someone whose life was prayer, and a door to God was opened which has never been completely closed ever since.

Just as we are changed by the presence of a praying person as we pray, just as we are changed by the presence of a living Christian community, so we are changed by the presence of the risen Lord at the Eucharist. None of us has arrived, we all continue in our need to be changed for the whole of our lives. We all have our own unique story to tell and each pair of empty hands, as they are held out to receive the sacrament, tells a different story. It is one of the great privileges of ordained ministry to know something of many of those stories, and the priest is always humbled as he comes to know the ordinary people of God. The change which takes place over the years, as each of us participates in the Eucharist, is sometimes known as secondary evangelism. In a missionary situation, primary evangelism is that which takes place from birth to baptism/conversion. The rest is secondary evangelism. It is about sanctification, the making holy of ordinary people. It has long been my conviction that whereas Evangelical

Christians tend to be good at primary evangelism, Catholic Christians are usually better at secondary evangelism. That is why Catholic and Evangelical are not alternatives, but need each other in order that the wholeness of the Gospel can be proclaimed.

(J.N.)

9

The Gift of Being Present

Evangelism is the bad news about the Good News. We all believe in evangelism, but no one wants to do it. Many Christians find this the hardest part of discipleship and get involved with extreme reluctance, usually because they are driven by guilt to do so. Guilt is a bad motive for evangelism; it creates fear and tension in situations where naturalness and friendliness are most called for.

A young man, who belonged to a strict Evangelical church, took seriously the church's policy, 'never to let a day go by without speaking to someone about Jesus'. One day he was on a train journey, alone in the carriage except for a very attractive woman who sat opposite. He had been unable up to this point in the day to find anyone with whom he could share his 'good news'. Feeling himself beginning to panic, he realised this would be the only likely opportunity for him to witness to his faith and so prove himself worthy of his church's approval. He imagined telling others at the prayer meeting of his bold adventures of faith. As the train sped to his destination, he rehearsed in his mind how he would set about his task. He knew he had a tract in his inside jacket pocket and convinced himself that the best way to witness on this occasion would be to give it to her, using some well-chosen words. By this time he was beginning to feel a bit tense. Suppose she became angry and rejected the gift of his tract. He was aware that it had been in his pocket for some time, and by now was a bit dog-eared. He began to get very anxious about the whole transaction. How could he reach into his pocket without drawing attention to himself? What form of words should he use to communicate the importance of his message? He had heard others in his fellowship testify as to how they had witnessed, heroically challenging their contacts about the state of their souls, and questioning them about where they would spend eternity. As he mulled over these thoughts he began to formulate his plan.

Meanwhile, the young lady sitting opposite became aware of the would-be evangelist with rising alarm. She observed his discomfort and the sweat on his brow. She noticed that from time to time he glanced furtively in her direction, occasionally slipping his hand into his inside jacket pocket. Out of the corner of her eye she had located the communication cord, and made the decision that she would scream loudly if he accosted her.

By now, of course, the train was rapidly approaching the station and the young man realised that if he was going to act he would have to move fast. Sweat poured from him, his mouth was dry, his heart began to pound as he rose half out of his seat to conclude his mission. Crouching over her and thrusting his hand into his inside pocket, his half-strangled voice choked out the words, 'Are you ready to die?' You can imagine the sequel.

This unnatural, and obviously forced, process does no good whatever. Sharing the good news has to do with our whole way of life, not merely with words, otherwise our efforts only add to the torrent of words washing through people's minds and have no effect whatever. Undoubtedly, we live in a word-resistant society in which the Church is being challenged to do more than pay lip-service to the faith. St Paul reminded the Christians at Thessalonica that the Gospel had been given to them, 'not simply with words, but also with power' (1 Thessalonians

1:5). The Christian community must be able to offer a more attractive way of life than most people on the whole experience. We have to face the fact that we may be a very long way from this possibility. Commenting ruefully on her experience of church life, a friend said that our first task is not to change people into Christians, but to change Christians into people.

THE EXAMPLE OF JESUS

It is refreshing to look at the gospels and observe Jesus, not only because he is always the finest example to follow, but also because he shows how to communicate in the most natural, and therefore the most effective ways. The problem with the young man on the train was that he was trying so hard to be super-natural that he became un-natural. The deepest possible meaning of the incarnation is that God ennobles and graces our human nature in such a way that it becomes the best vehicle for the 'Divine Word'. It is possible, therefore, that our humanness is the most effective form of communication to fellow human-beings. Grace does not cancel out human nature, rather it transforms it so that, even in our sinfulness, we become the 'presence' of Christ to our generation. The word needs to be clothed with flesh to make it heard.

One of the ways in which St John chooses to introduce Jesus is by recounting the first miracle that he did in Cana of Galilee, when he turned water into wine. Apart from being a key sign of the coming of Christ, it beautifully demonstrated the Word becoming flesh, the divine working through the human. The story is very familiar. There was a wedding to which Jesus and the disciples were invited. A potentially embarrassing situation emerged when it was discovered that they were running out of wine at this important family celebration. Jesus' mother, as many mothers would, was keen to thrust her son into the limelight, and so encouraged him to do something about it. What was in her mind is impossible to say, except that she was bound, at this stage, to have some inkling of her son's extraordinary abilities. After some delay Jesus instructed the caterers to fill with water six stone jars, each one holding between twenty and thirty gallons. When it was drawn it was discovered to be wine of the finest quality. Just think of it, between 120 and 180 gallons of good quality wine – it must have been a brilliant party!

Fascinatingly, St John records the occasion as one where Jesus revealed his glory, a consequence of which was that his disciples came to faith. It might be tempting to think that it was the miracle that was the most important part of this event, but I wonder if that was the case. Other aspects seem to have equal, if not greater, significance. Consider not only the miraculous but also the ordinary components of the story, not only the ultimate but also the proximate realities. Jesus, as good friend and neighbour, attended a wedding. It was undoubtedly a special event, but set within the context of the ordinariness of the affairs of family and community. His host ran out of wine, embarrassing enough at the best of times but painfully so at a wedding. Consider also a social context in which hospitality was very important and deeply symbolic. To give a person clothing you give them something to wear, to give them food and drink you give them something to make them live. Hospitality is life-giving. It was a matter, therefore, of considerable anxiety to this newly married couple that they should have run out of wine at their wedding celebration. They would have felt ashamed and embarrassed, not only because of a failure to offer adequate hospitality to their guests, but also because they would consider it a bad sign at the beginning of their new life together. Jesus, out of sheer concern for the embarrassment of his hosts, acted to make practical provision for them, but he did it with a richness and generosity that made them feel special. ' "Everyone brings out the choice wine first and then the cheaper wine after the guests have had too much to drink; but you have saved the best till now" ' (John 2:10). One could spiritualise this incident and talk about the wine of the Spirit, but I actually think that it is the presence of Christ in the ordinariness of day-to-day life that is the most exciting part of this story. Jesus' presence made so much possible. Being present for others is the most powerful statement of the Gospel imaginable. Being there for people gives us unlimited opportunity to share the love of Christ, not only in the words we use, but in the Christlikeness of our actions. At a church meeting where evangelism was being discussed, an old lady was heard to say that she didn't think she was up to the task of preaching the Gospel. All she could do, and in fact had been doing for years, was to bake for neighbours who were ill or housebound. Her presence in that neighbourhood made evangelism real, because she earned the right for the Church to speak. Through her wordless love the Divine Word became flesh and dwelt amongst her neighbours. It was in his practical love for the couple at the wedding that the glory of Christ was revealed. The implications for us are enormous, transforming every act of service and love into a revelation of the presence of Jesus.

THE HOPE OF 'BEING'

God created us as human beings, not human 'doings'. This rather simplistic statement contains an important truth. It is not only that God values us for who we are more than for what we do, but that the mysteries of God are revealed in 'being', and through our humanness. The story is told of a holy man on a journey. Reaching the outskirts of a village he settled down under a tree for the night, when a villager came running up to him shouting, 'The stone! The stone! Give me the precious stone!' 'What stone?' asked the holy man. 'Last night an angel appeared to me in a dream,' explained the villager, 'and told me to go to the outskirts of the village at dusk where I would meet a man who would give me a precious stone that would make me very rich.' The holy man rummaged in his bag and pulled out a stone. 'He must have meant this one,' he said as he handed over the stone to the villager. 'I found it on my path some days ago. Here, take it.' The man gazed at the stone in wonder. It was a diamond, as big as his hand. The lucky villager took the stone gratefully and walked away. All night he tossed and turned in bed, unable to sleep. Very early next day, he went back to where the holy man was camped and woke him up. 'Please,' he said, 'give me the wealth that enables you to give this valuable diamond away so easily.' Christianity is about the discovery of a hidden treasure far more valuable than precious stones. The possession of this treasure enables us to make choices, and order our priorities, according to a completely different set of values from those that dictate the actions and attitudes of most people. Such a discovery makes explicit our discipleship, and bears silent witness to the living Christ.

The formation of discipleship in which Jesus is free to mould and shape us, and make us into real 'beings' is our most powerful evangelistic tool. He was present for others in a way which simultaneously made them feel both loved and challenged. His unconditional love is, however, like no other love. It lacks all the limitations of human love, because it exists entirely and completely for the good of the one loved. For us to be transformed by that love creates within us a compelling motive to share it with others. Frequently, the Church gives the impression that it is interested in people only for what it can get out of them. This clearly negates the whole of the Gospel, and establishes traditions of suspicion for every generation, thus making our task of evangelism so much more difficult. To be the 'presence' of Christ for others is the greatest possible privilege, and sets us free from the driven need to take spiritual scalps.

A friend of mine, who is a roofer by trade, became a Christian largely through the silent witness of another friend. When I was vicar of a city-centre church we embarked on a huge project to rebuild the adjacent derelict school building. The leadership of the church believed it was right to do most of the rebuilding work ourselves with teams of voluntary labour from the church. In a large congregation there were many of the relevant skills, and those which we did not possess could be bought in. The two-storey building had to be gutted before being rebuilt. Part of the plan was to reshape the roof and reslate it. We employed a local skilled roofer to do the job, who did what he had to do and then stayed on to help as a volunteer. He had been impressed by the quality of life of one of the church members who worked as a team leader. This man's life had so moved him that it began the process which led to him coming to faith. There had been no preaching, no pressure, no spiritual hints and innuendos, merely the quality of a life that revealed the presence of Christ. One man enabled Jesus to be present for another. In this way the Word was made flesh, and the miracle of new birth occurred. It seems to me that there is hope in this for all of us.

FRIENDSHIP – THE CONTEXT
FOR PROCLAMATION

None of this, of course, rules out the need to say something. The good news has to be proclaimed. What we have done up to now is to begin to establish a context in which the greatest news of all might be heard. Who do we listen to most of all? Our friends. The vast majority of people who come to faith, do so because of a friendship. In friendship we open ourselves to others so that they can test, in all kinds of different circumstances, the authenticity of our faith. Our friends will test readily enough whether our mouths, hearts and eyes speak the same language. Proclamation, without practising our faith, is simply posturing. It is therefore in friendship that the most important truths about ourselves are shared. Our friends will know whether our faith works, or whether it is simply a casual hobby to be entertained if there is time and sufficient interest. This does not mean we have to be perfect. Sometimes the most powerful statements are made about faith without us knowing it, for instance when faced with failure or doubt, or when confronted by painful human circumstances. If our faith makes a difference to us in adverse circumstances, we are given the right to speak about the hope that is in us. The means of communication, however, is friendship. This is the route along which all important realities are shared. Jesus, when he called the disciples, invited them into friendship with him. 'I have called you friends, for everything that I learned from my Father I have made known to you' (John 15:15). He drew people close to him so that they could share in his life, and incidentally, this provided the most effective form of training to prepare them for future ministry. This is so simple and so obvious, it is amazing that Christians do not more readily enter into it. Instead, we produce programmes and techniques for evangelism that require immense amounts of energy to sustain. Friendship, the natural gift of being human, is to be the means through which the kingdom of God will be established. Friendship and encouragement are two of the most important ministries accessible to all, and are also two of the most fruitful. They are the ultimate in cost-effectiveness because they are completely free.

Sometimes, the power of friendship, implicit in the Gospel, is seen more clearly by those outside Christianity. A young male Muslim, talking to the aged Michael Ramsey, asked him how long he had been ordained. 'Sixty years,' the Archbishop replied. After a moment's thought the young man said, 'That is a very long friendship.' Significantly, he had seen that ordination was to do with friendship with God. Long before professional ministry can be seen as a skill, it must be experienced as friendship with God. This sets the tone for the whole creative operation of ministry, and serves as a reminder that ministry is about making friends. Introducing others into friendship with Jesus by means of our own friendship with them, is the great privilege of Christian ministry.

What we say about our faith in Christ will then occur within the spontaneous outworking of our friendships, where others will sense our commitment to them as people, and will therefore be able to hear what we are saying. Making people feel guilty is not our job; making them feel loved is. When Jesus attended the wedding at Cana in Galilee, he went as a guest to celebrate this family event. His commitment was seen in his presence, and because he was 'present' he was able to demonstrate love. If we did no more than encourage our friends to come to faith, the Church would experience phenomenal growth. But as we share our faith with our friends, we become less concerned with the statistics of Church growth, and much more concerned with the total well-being of those who are our friends. It could be that the most effective way of proclaiming the Gospel is to allow the genuineness of our faith to emerge through our friendships, so that Christ can be 'present' to others in us.

(C.A.)

10

The Supremacy of Love

> Love is patient, love is kind. It does not envy, it does not boast, it is not proud. It is not rude, it is not self-seeking, it is not easily angered, it keeps no record of wrongs. Love does not delight in evil but rejoices with the truth. It always protects, always trusts, always hopes, always perseveres. Love never fails. (1 Corinthians 13:4–8)

The finest and most perceptive Christian truths are summed up in these few verses. It is ultimately lack of love that destroys people, and it is love, and love alone, that makes them whole. Jesus exemplified love. Everything about him spoke of love. Whether people heard his voice, received his touch, looked in his eyes, or felt the warmth of his heart, they got the same message. They knew they were loved, and that love made them whole. It is this love the Church has the great privilege to share with others. When Jesus meets with us, the first thing he sees is not our sin, but the infinitely redeemable beauty of a person made in the image of God. In our heart of hearts we know that the people who help us most are not the holiest, or the cleverest, or the youngest, or the oldest, or the wisest, but the ones who love us unconditionally. Jesus was not a trained therapist or counsellor, nor even a trained priest. He transformed people because he loved them. He was, and is, the exemplar of the truths revealed in the above verses about love.

This chapter provides a brief sampling of the early chapters of St John's gospel in an attempt to demonstrate how Jesus put this love into practice. He is Lord of the Church and offers us the grace of love with which we can reach out and be agents of transformation for others. When we study the life of Jesus, and especially the way he treated people, a number of factors in his approach immediately become obvious.

RESPECT FOR THE INDIVIDUAL

Whether one looks at the wedding of Cana in Galilee (John 2:1–11), the incident with Nicodemus (John 3:1–21), or the discussions with the woman of Samaria (John 4:1–26), Jesus is seen to treat individuals with great respect. Many of the qualities of love mentioned in 1 Corinthians 13 are summed up in this one important factor in relationships, respect for the individual. His kindness to the young couple at the wedding, his patience with Nicodemus who came to see him under cover of darkness, and his gentle sensitivity to the woman at the well: all speak of his consideration for the person involved. He could of course be angry when confronted by extortion and injustice, as the incident of the clearing of the Temple indicated (John 2:12–25). He could also be confrontational when the need arose, as revealed in his challenge to Nicodemus to be born again. But the overriding motive for his actions was always that of respect.

Consider the way he attended to the woman at the well in Samaria. Not only was he prepared to cross all the religious, cultural, social and political boundaries in order to speak to her, but also he was prepared to put his reputation at risk. She had lived an extremely colourful life having been married five times, and was currently living with someone else. Nevertheless, we get the distinct impression that she was, for Jesus at that moment, the most important person in the world. He entered into debate with her, considered her views and took seriously her comments. In pastoral ministry it is very easy to be patronising and dismissive, especially when in contact with people who are disadvantaged, or whose views would not normally be sought on important matters. Jesus, however, in a quite staggering reversal of roles, put himself in the place of need, and her in the place of power. He asked her to give him a drink. In the market-place of human worth where her experience up until now would have been entirely negative, this immediately gave her dignity, value and respect. She was the person with something to offer. Because we are all made in the image of God, every person is holy ground and therefore deserves to be approached with love and respect.

A colleague, who worked as a chaplain in a hospital which housed many long-term patients with severe mental disabilities, taught me key lessons in pastoral care. No matter who he was with, and whether the patient could communicate or not, he gave the person his full attention. We have probably all been with people who, when talking to us, are constantly looking around to see if they can catch the eye of anyone more important to talk to. It leaves you with the feeling that you are not really worth much. This chaplain never acted in this way, and I find myself thinking often about the Christlikeness of his manner.

WILLINGNESS TO LISTEN

One of the earlier chapters in this book is about telling your story. Everyone has a story, and longs to tell it to someone and have it understood and accepted. To listen, with attention and respect, to someone's story is to give them a gift of great value. Every human being has a history, which is both sacred and fragile. When a person begins to open up there is a process of exploration going on. Will the hearer be shocked at the things that may emerge? Will he or she be judgemental or critical? Will the listener be able to hear the things that remain unsaid, as well as the things that are spoken? There is probably no greater act of love in the realm of human relationships than to be a good listener. When children are young, parents can decide more freely when to spend time listening. As the children get older, *they* decide when they want to talk. The skill we need to cultivate is that of knowing when to drop everything we are doing and spend time listening. Frequently, someone will take a long time to decide who is trustworthy, and who will listen with patience and respect. But the moment they choose to want to talk may well be very inconvenient for the listener. Nicodemus, a member of the Jewish ruling council, needed to talk. No doubt he had been weighing Jesus up for some time, considering carefully the risks involved in being seen talking to him. So he came to Jesus at night. Jesus listened to him without compromising him or mocking his desire for secrecy. They debated important spiritual issues which resulted in some straight talking about this Pharisee's spiritual needs.

Listening takes time, and the time chosen by the one who needs to talk may not always be convenient. It demands being fully present and attentive for as long as it takes, putting aside our own needs and concerns. Listening will touch the sources of our own pain, and will often make us feel completely helpless. Our own sorrows will be raked over mercilessly, and our convictions called into question as we listen to the stories of others. The speaker may not be attractive, may be dull and self-centred, and may make demands difficult to meet. Nevertheless, the sheer grace of God enables us to offer the gift of listening. It is an act of love. Above all, it is an act which has within it the power to bring wholeness.

LOVE KEEPS NO RECORD OF WRONGS

A married couple were having an argument. 'Why is it', he asked, 'that you constantly remind me of my faults? I thought you had forgiven and forgotten.' 'I have,' she replied, 'but I don't want you to forget that I have forgiven and forgotten.' One of the primary aspects of Christ's love is that it keeps no record of wrongs. When he spoke to the woman at the well in Samaria, he did not keep on reminding her of her sins. Nor when he attended the wedding in Cana did he remind the hosts of their failure to provide enough wine. Similarly, when he spoke to the religious leader Nicodemus, he did not rebuke him for his failure to get himself sorted out spiritually. Jesus kept no record of the failures, wrongs and sins of others. That, above all, is a characteristic of genuine love for the person.

When we pray in the Lord's Prayer, 'Forgive us our sins as we forgive those who sin against us', we are actually praying that we will be enabled to 'let go' of our sin. Forgiveness means letting go. When we read the word forgiveness in the New Testament, it is most commonly a translation of the Greek word *aphesis*, which simply means 'letting go'. This word expresses accurately what Jesus himself said he had come to do. He came to release people from their sins and burdens, as though setting them free from a prison. He came to set us free from death. When Lazarus was called out of the tomb, bystanders were invited to share in the work of *aphesis*. 'Loose him,' said Jesus, 'and let him go.'

As Jesus lets go of our sins and wrongdoing, so he

expects us to forgive, or 'let go', the sins of others. Many of us are, however, theoretical about forgiveness. We know it is a good idea, and applaud it as an important Christian truth, but almost always think of it in the context of other people's responsibility to forgive *us*. Forgiveness is a good idea until *we* have something to forgive. Many people cling to hurts that have been inflicted on them, and can remember in vivid detail offences that have been committed against them. However, in so doing they make themselves the prisoner. We need to let go of other people's sins against us, because unless we do we ourselves become imprisoned, clinging on to their offences and allowing them to rule, and ruin, our lives. The love of Christ keeps no record of wrongs. This does not necessarily mean that we can no longer remember offences committed against us, but that they do not have any power over us, and we are free to go on loving the person. To keep a record of another's wrongs is to condemn both them and us to a form of imprisonment. As Christ has let go of our sins, so we should try to let go of the sins of others. Occasionally a symbolic act may help us to do this. Write down the sins that you have asked to be forgiven, or the offences and sins that have been committed against you. Pray over the list, telling God that you are willing to let them all go, and then burn the piece of paper. This is an act of letting go which symbolically destroys the record of wrongs that you have committed, and also those that have been committed against you. Love keeps no record of wrongs. Thereafter, when guilt, anger, or resentment rise up within you in relation to any of those offences, you can remind yourself that the record is destroyed.

THE CHURCH – A HOSPITABLE COMMUNITY

In the Decade of Evangelism an icon which has had a significant impact on a great number of people is Rublev's 'Hospitality of Abraham'. There are three figures sitting round a table, with spaces in between them to include those who wish to draw near. The icon is about welcome and hospitality, and its overriding mood is a desire to include the worshipper, and even the onlooker, in the very frame of the icon iself. The icon painter interprets the text from Genesis 18. Abraham is about to settle down for a midday sleep when three men appear. Immediately he offers them the hospitality of his home, and he does so with characteristic generosity. To begin with, Abraham accepts the obvious fact that he is entertaining three travellers, but later realises that it is the Lord who is visiting him. Early Christian writers saw this incident as a foreshadowing of the later revelation in the New Testament of the Holy Trinity. Rublev captures, with breaktaking vividness, the openness of the three figures, and gives us a powerful image of hospitality. The icon invites us to enter the very circle composed of the Father, the Son, and the Holy Spirit. In an act of utter love we are included in the hospitality of heaven.

As the incident with Abraham revealed his overwhelming generosity to his visitors, so Rublev's icon speaks of the generosity of God. Each living human being has a place in the love of God. Jesus, who is 'the Way', invites us to take our place in the community of heaven. The Church, which is the visible and touchable presence of the Body of Christ, must have hospitality as the very essence of its life. Everything about us must invite people in to experience, through our love, the overwhelmingly generous love of God. We are to be an icon for the hospitality of heaven. Open doors and open hearts are the symbols of such hospitality. It is time for the Church to restate its priorities, especially that of making known to all the love of God as revealed in Jesus, and inviting our neighbours, through our human community, to experience the community of heaven.

> If I speak in the tongues of men and of angels, but have not love, I am only a resounding gong or a clanging cymbal. If I have the gift of prophecy and can fathom all mysteries and all knowledge, and if I have faith that can move mountains, but have not love, I am nothing. If I give all I possess to the poor and surrender my body to the flames, but have not love, I gain nothing. . . . Love never fails. (1 Corinthians 13:1–3, 8)

(C.A.)

We Believe – Exploring and Living the Creed Today

This is a seven-week course for small groups to explore their faith. Based on the Nicene Creed, the course was written by lay people for lay people. It is intended that the course should build confidence and encourage people, both in knowing what they believe and in their willingness to share their faith with others. The stress is on informality, participation and enjoyment. It is written in simple English and related to our everyday lives. Each session is designed to last for approximately one and a half hours.

Throughout the course there is an expectation that God will speak to us and help us grow in faith through sharing experience. The final study directs the church towards mission.

Group leaders are to be enablers rather than teachers. A distinctive feature of the course is co-leadership. Each group needs two leaders, and a training weekend plan for leaders is to be found in Appendix 2.

If your parish would like to use this course:

1. Decide how many groups it is feasible to set up. The optimum size for the group will be between eight and ten people.
2. From each group choose two people who ideally will go on a training weekend and afterwards lead the group.

A number of parishes in the diocese of Blackburn did a trial run, and their response has been very encouraging. Here are some of the comments made by participants:

> This course tremendously increased my belief and my ability to talk more openly to others about what I believe.

> This can be a recipe for growth both individually and for the Church at large.

> It made me reread sections of my Bible I had forgotten and question and reassess some of my views.

> I was stimulated to read more widely and think in greater depth about our faith.

> An excellent course – more please!

> I particularly enjoyed discussing the Christian faith and having the opportunity to bring up certain points which I had found difficult to understand.

> It has been a great source of learning and inspiration.

> The sheer diversity of thought and experience revealed in this group has greatly enlarged my view and understanding of other Christians and our work as the Body of Christ.

> It was lovely and quite moving at times.

THE NICENE CREED

We believe in one God,
the Father, the almighty,
maker of heaven and earth,
of all that is,
seen and unseen.

We believe in one Lord, Jesus Christ,
the only Son of God,
eternally begotten of the Father,

God from God, Light from Light,
true God from true God,
begotten, not made,
of one Being with the Father.
Through him all things were made.
For us men and our salvation
he came down from heaven;
by the power of the Holy Spirit
he became incarnate of the Virgin
    Mary, and was made man.
For our sake he was crucified under
    Pontius Pilate;
he suffered death and was buried.
On the third day he rose again
in accordance with the Scriptures;
he ascended into heaven
and is seated at the right hand of the
    Father.
He will come again in glory
to judge the living and the dead,
and his kingdom will have no end.

We believe in the Holy Spirit,
the Lord, the giver of life,
who proceeds from the Father and Son.
With the Father and the Son he is
worshipped and glorified.
He has spoken through the Prophets.

We believe in one holy catholic and
    apostolic Church.
We acknowledge one baptism for the
    forgiveness of sins.
We look for the resurrection of the
dead, and the life of the world
to come.

                                        AMEN.

Contents of course

SESSION 1 – IN THE BEGINNING

We believe in one God,
the Father, the almighty,
maker of heaven and earth,
of all that is,
seen and unseen.

Key learning points

1. God created everything and it was good.
2. We are all created to know God in an intimate way.
3. For this relationship to be real, we must choose to be in it.
4. Turning away from God is sin.

Welcome

Introduce the programme format and any domestic details.

Icebreaker

A 10–20 minute exercise (allow 1–2 minutes per group member for sharing). This activity is designed to help members get to know each other.

Suggestions: 'Three things I'd like you to know about me.'

Begin by giving the others an example. Some ideas might include sharing how long you have attended the church, something about your family, a favourite thing to do, a favourite food, a place to visit, a hobby, etc. To close this activity note how different we all are; no two people have had exactly the same kinds of experiences with the same reactions; no one looks or has dressed exactly alike. There is a great diversity present in the group.

Share

Try to encourage group members to share an example or experience of when they have been aware of the creative presence of God. Be prepared to share an experience you have had. Allow approximately five minutes for this. Some members may not wish to share.

Pray

A brief prayer to emphasise a sense of expectation. Ask that God will speak to the group through the reading.

Bible texts that could be used

Genesis 1:1–2:3; Genesis 3:1–13; Genesis 3:21; Genesis 6:6–9; 1 John 1:1–2; Luke 3:21–2.

Read

Genesis 1:1–2:3. Because this is a lengthy passage, it is important that it be well read, with expression. Ideally it should be read by one person, someone other than the leaders if possible.

Questions to stimulate discussion
(Allow approximately 50–60 minutes)

1. As we review the first chapter of Genesis, we see God's handiwork. How does he show his care and concern in creation? (Emphasise the awesomeness of creation, its many aspects, our uniqueness, etc.)

2. What does Genesis 1:31 reveal about God's character? ('It was very good' – God is good; the orderliness of

creation; a divine plan.) What qualities do you see in God as he gives over responsibility for his creation to humankind? (Emphasise God's generosity. He entrusted us with stewardship of the earth. Issues of ownership over against stewardship.)

3. What kind of relationship did God want to have with Adam and Eve? (Fellowship with them, an intimate relationship, spending time with them talking face to face, a love relationship.)

4. Why do you think God gave us a free will when so much is at stake? What would have happened if we had not been given a free will? (We have the option to choose, the underpinning of creation. We need this choice to move into the intimate relationship which God desires to have with us.)

5. Read Genesis 3:1–13. Describe the events surrounding the downfall of Adam and Eve. What pitfalls still exist for us today? (Identify the stages of sin:
   (a) questioning, doubt/temptation,
   (b) challenging what God has said – deception/ delusion,
   (c) desiring,
   (d) acting.

   Some may make comments about Eve and the fall being woman's fault. Emphasise that they both sinned and were equally guilty. You may note the similarities in the way they responded to temptation.) From the passage we have just read, could we come up with a definition of sin? (Sin is often referred to as 'missing the mark', disobedience.)

6. Before Adam and Eve were driven out of the garden, what do we see God do? Let's look at Genesis 3:21. What does this say about the nature of God? (Grace, care, provision.)

7. What are the consequences of sin for Adam and Eve, for us today? (God has people's best interest at heart.

We set up ways of living which value things, possessions, more than people; ways of living where we fail to love our brothers and sisters, e.g. racial prejudice. Our relationships are divided and conflict soon occurs. Sin sets aside obedience, God's best plan for us, for disobedience, our plan for ourselves. Disregarding God's plan, we set ourselves higher than God. It always leads to conflict – and, if left unchecked, destruction and death. This destruction and death can happen in every area of our lives: emotionally, mentally, physically, spiritually, etc.)

8. How does Genesis 6:6–9 describe God's response to sin? (Anger, grief, compassion, desire for relationship with human beings.)

9. Can we identify aspects of the fatherhood of God at work in this study? (As has been stated earlier, we see God's provision, care, compassion, protection . . . all at work in this study.)

To close

Read together the Collect for the Ninth Sunday before Christmas.

COLLECT FOR NINTH SUNDAY BEFORE CHRISTMAS

Almighty God,
you have created the heavens and the earth
and made man in your own image.
Teach us to discern your hand in all your
    works,
and to serve you with reverence and
    thanksgiving;
through Jesus Christ our Lord,
who with you and the Holy Spirit
reigns supreme over all things
now and forever.

                    AMEN.

SESSION 2 – MEEKNESS AND MAJESTY

We believe in one Lord, Jesus Christ,
the only Son of God,
eternally begotten of the Father,
God from God, Light from Light,
true God from true God,
begotten, not made,
of one Being with the Father.
Through him all things were made.
For us men and our salvation
he came down from heaven;
by the power of the Holy Spirit
he became incarnate of the Virgin Mary,
and was made man.

Key learning points

1. Divinity, pre-existence of Jesus.
2. Son of Man, humanity of Jesus – a person like you and me.
3. Ministry of Jesus.

Welcome

Take care of any practical details; introduce the theme for the study.

Icebreaker

You may remember last session when we shared three things about ourselves with the group. This week let's tell the group three more things about ourselves, but this time only two of them are true. As each individual shares, the rest of the group attempts to decide which is untrue. The leader should begin and set an enjoyable tone.

Pray

For guidance, wisdom and understanding.

Bible texts that could be used

Luke 5:17–26; Luke 8:42b–8; Mark 10:32–4,45; 1 John 1:1–2; Hebrews 1:1–3.

Questions to stimulate discussion

(Allow 50–60 minutes)

1. What was your first impression of Jesus, whenever you first heard about him or experienced him? Try to think of one word to describe him as you experienced him then. Could you share that with the group? (Gentle, meek, etc.) As time has passed, has your picture changed? Can you think of one other word which you feel would describe your experience of him now? (Powerful, revolutionary, etc.)

2. Read Luke 5:17–26. As we read, imagine you are there. Let's view this scene from four perspectives: those of (1) the sick man, (2) the friends, (3) the Pharisees and teachers of the law, (4) the onlookers. (Ask the members to select one from the above and try to share that perspective.)

3. Let's look at the principles at work in this passage. What was the first thing Jesus responded to? (Faith.) What did he do in response to this? (Forgave the man's sins.) Why would this place Jesus in conflict with the Pharisees? (Only God could forgive sin.) How did Jesus prove his authority? (He told the man to take up his mat and walk, and the man did. As you go through these questions, do it naturally rather than 'reading through'. Allow time for members to reflect on Jesus as Son of God and Son of Man at work in this passage.)

4. Do you feel that the order of these events is significant and important for us today? (Key points here to draw out:
   (a) Jesus responds to faith, whether it be that of our friends or our own.

    (b) God knows the times when we struggle to believe.

    (c) He cares for us by providing others to pray on our behalf. The lame man, bound to his mat, is a perfect picture of what it means to carry a burden to the Lord. The friends knew that Christ was able to heal him and they didn't let any obstacles get in their way. They were determined to reach Christ.)

5. What was the reaction of the man and the crowd to what they had experienced? What happens to our faith when we experience God at work? (Amazement, thankfulness, and wanting to tell others – testimony. This is an ideal opportunity for one or two people to share an experience.)

6. Another example of Jesus' ministry is in Luke 8:42b–8. Why did the woman tremble when Jesus asked who touched him? Why was she frightened? (Leviticus 15:27: 'Whoever touches them will be unclean'. She was a social outcast and anyone who touched her would become unclean and an outcast as well.)

7. What was the process Jesus was trying to reveal to the crowd? (Jesus knew someone had touched him, for power had left him. He wanted the woman to admit to touching him so that he could recognise her faith, make it public, and demonstrate his authority through healing her.)

8. Read Mark 10:32–4,45. The same man who has demonstrated great power and authority, saying that he is God, is now saying he is going to be killed. What in these verses is revealed about his purpose? (He is ahead of them, walking to Jerusalem, knowing what is in store. The servant leader, willing to give his life as a ransom for many, is prepared to die for our sake.)

9. How is Jesus' divine nature reflected in the passages we have just looked at? What parallels can we see between Jesus' behaviour and that of God in creation? (Grace, compassion, love, authority, power, power to achieve goodness, his desire for our wholeness; he related to each person uniquely according to their need.)

10. Looking at the Creed, does it surprise you to read that Jesus was present at the creation? Read 1 John 1:1–2; Hebrews 1:1–3. (This may be a new idea for some.)

Pray

We have been looking at Jesus in action. Could we offer a brief prayer of thanks to him, a phrase or sentence with a leader beginning and giving an example. Ask who would be willing to close the prayer.

COLLECT FOR THIRD SUNDAY AFTER EPIPHANY

Almighty God,
Whose Son revealed in signs and miracles
the wonder of your saving love;
renew your people with your heavenly
grace,
and in all our weakness
sustain us by your mighty power;
through Jesus Christ our Lord.

AMEN.

SESSION 3 – FOR OUR SAKE

For our sake he was crucified
under Pontius Pilate;
he suffered death and was buried.

Key learning points

1. An understanding of why Jesus had to die for us.
2. Our response to that.
3. The nature of forgiveness.

Welcome

Take care of any practical details; introduce the study.

Pray

A brief prayer asking for wisdom to understand God's love and the price he is prepared to pay for that love.

Bible texts that could be used

Romans 5:6–10; Isaiah 53:7–12.

Questions to stimulate discussion
(Allow 50–60 minutes)

1. Can you remember a time when you were moved by the cross, a symbol of God's love? (Draw out different experiences, examples from the group. Remember, not every member may wish to share.)
2. Read Romans 5:6–10. Do you consider that you are an enemy of God? (Some members may have difficulty with the passage; they may have never thought of themselves in this light. Draw out why we would be considered enemies.)
3. Another word for 'enemy' is 'transgressor'. Jesus said of himself, 'It is written: "And he was numbered with the transgressors"; and I tell you that this must be fulfilled in me' (Luke 22:37). Now read Isaiah 53:7–12. How did Jesus see himself? (Jesus was the servant who was to suffer to bring God's people back to his love. Draw out the parallels between the Isaiah passage and Jesus' trial, flogging and crucifixion.)
4. Jesus also said, 'This is the blood of the covenant which is poured out for many for the forgiveness of sins' (Matthew 26:28). These words are the source of our communion services each week. What does it mean to

you to receive the bread and wine? There could be many different responses here. Encourage sharing from those who are willing; listen for those who may have difficulties, e.g. drinking blood, God's need for sacrifices.)

5. What helps you most to accept God's forgiveness?

6. In the communion service we say the Lord's Prayer. We ask for God's forgiveness and say that we have forgiven others. Listen to this story and consider the following questions. (Read: 'Gordon and Joan Wilson can't find it in their hearts or their faith to hate anyone, even the bombers who brought horror to Remembrance Sunday in Enniskillen', *Scottish Catholic Observer*. The Wilsons' 21–year-old daughter, Marie, was tragically killed in that awful Remembrance Day blast. The press-cutting just read was a typical reaction in the wake of the Wilsons' stated forgiveness of their daughter's killers. Many people admire Gordon Wilson for his reaction but others find it infuriating.

    (a) What helps us manage to forgive people who hurt us or our families?

    (b) Why is forgiveness so important?

    (c) Do we sometimes find it difficult to forgive ourselves? Why?

7. Does our church show itself as a forgiving community? If so, how? If not, how should it?

To close

Sing, pray or say 'When I survey the wondrous cross'.

SESSION 4 – WHAT'S NEXT?

On the third day he rose again
in accordance with the Scriptures;
he ascended into heaven

and is seated at the right hand of
the Father.
He will come again in glory
to judge the living and the dead,
and his kingdom will have no end.

Key learning points

1. We are being transformed by the death and resurrection of Christ.
2. We are challenged to discover his kingdom in new ways.

Welcome

Introduce the study and any practical details.

Pray

A brief prayer that the group will meet the risen Jesus.

Bible texts that could be used

Luke 24:36–43; Luke 24:52–3; Matthew 13:44–6; Matthew 13:47–52; John 14:1–4.

Questions to stimulate discussion
(Allow 50–60 minutes)

1. Imagine you have spent the last two years of your life as a disciple following Christ. You listened as he taught you many things. You saw him perform many miracles. You were with him when he rode into Jerusalem as a triumphant king. You watched as he was taken captive and executed. How do you feel? (Emphasise the confusion, betrayal, fear, hurt and feelings of being misled and/or cheated.)
2. Scripture gives many accounts of Jesus visiting the disciples after he rose from the dead. Read Luke 24:36–43. What struggle did the disciples have with the resurrection? (Disbelief, fear.) Is this a struggle for us today? Why is the resurrection such good news? (Freedom from sin, proof of God's love.)

3. Read John 20:19–20. When Jesus came to the disciples, how did he find them? (Locked away together, in fear, wondering what to do next.) How did Jesus' presence change them? (They were filled with peace, joy.) Have you ever drawn comfort from knowing Jesus was with you, even though at some level you might have been struggling to believe? (Draw out the same contrast the disciples experience between fear and peace, and that Jesus came to the disciples at the height of their fear and uncertainty. His presence with them broke through their unbelief, encouraging them to believe. When we experience Jesus in our lives, our faith grows.)

4. The fact that Jesus was alive changed the way the disciples behaved – how? Read Luke 24:36,37 and contrast it with Luke 24:52,53. (Draw out the change from being fearful, locked away, inward-looking, to a public display of worship and praise at the very heart of the establishment that they feared.)

5. What in our behaviour would convince an observer that we are being transformed by the death and resurrection of Jesus? (Draw out the similarities with the disciples, i.e. we go to church, have fellowship, worship, begin to change habits, share things, look after each other, build up loving relationships, react differently towards death, are bold enough to share our faith with others.)

6. In the Nicene Creed we say, 'his kingdom will have no end.' Let's look at three of Jesus' parables about the kingdom of heaven. In Matthew 13:44–6 there are two parables about discovering the kingdom.

   (a) What is different about the way the man in the field and the merchant discovered their treasures? (The man in the field probably stumbled upon the treasure, not knowing that it was there. But once found, he knew the value of the treasure and went to buy it so he wouldn't lose it. Buying the field cost him everything he owned. The pearl merchant, on the other hand, was looking for a pearl of great value, and when he discovered the bargain, sold everything he had to buy it.)

(b) What do you think we need to 'sell' in order to 'buy' the kingdom of heaven?

(c) What kinds of things do we hold on to which prevent us from making this purchase?

(d) In Matthew 13:47–52 there is another parable of the kingdom. What is symbolised by the fishermen, the valuable and worthless fish?

(e) How do you feel when you see Jesus in the role of judge?

7. Read John 14:1–4. These verses are often given as a comfort to those who have been bereaved. How should our belief in them affect our living? (Jesus has prepared a place for us with him. That brings us comfort, hope and encouragement. It shows once again his concern for us. It reminds us that we, as believers, know the way to him. This is good news that we will want to share with others.)

8. When we say as Christians that our hope is in God, what do we mean? Can we explain our hope to others? To what extent is God's love for us part of the answer?

Pray

As we come to the close of this study, Lord, help us to thank you for the many ways you have taken care of us. (As leader, give an example yourself, and then ask each group member to offer up something. Allow time for individuals to respond and then close by thanking him for the greatest gift of all which he gave to us – that of himself.)

SESSION 5 – THE LIFE-GIVING SPIRIT

We believe in the Holy Spirit,
the Lord, the giver of life,
who proceeds from the Father and the Son.
With the Father and the Son he is
worshipped and glorified.
He has spoken through the Prophets.

Key learning points

1. An understanding of who and what the Holy Spirit is and what he does.
2. The Spirit is for everybody.
3. The Spirit is active now.

Welcome

Take care of any practical details and introduce the study.

Pray

A brief prayer that the group will recognise the Holy Spirit in their daily lives.

Bible texts that could be used

Genesis 1:2; Judges 3:9–11; 1 Samuel 10:9–13; Acts 2:14; John 14:15–17; John 16:5–15; 1 Corinthians 12:4–11; Galatians 5:22–5.

Questions to stimulate discussion

(Allow 50–60 minutes)

1. What comes into your mind when you think of the Holy Spirit? (This will be a brainstorming time when people offer ideas. Get them started by sharing a word, phrase or visual image, and why you think of this. Some ideas include: fire, wind, dove, teacher, counsellor, etc. Depending on the group, you may either use a large sheet of paper and write down comments which could be put up for all to see, or you could use separate

pieces of paper which could be put together on a large piece of card to make a collage. Use about 5–10 minutes to brainstorm. You may want to use this again at the end of the study to help summarise.)

2. Has the Spirit been active throughout the ages? How do the following passages show the Spirit at work? (Read one at a time and discuss briefly.)

   (a) Genesis 1:2 (creative element).

   (b) Judges 3:9–11 (empowering, Othniel's role changed and the eventual result was peace).

   (c) 1 Samuel 10:9–13 (empowering with a specific gift which became a witness to others – an example of prophecy).

   (d) Acts 2:14 Peter (empowering with a specific gift to preach and a boldness to do it in the heart of the city, despite the danger this would mean).

   (e) John Wesley – before and after (after years of sensing that there was something more and praying for this, his life and ministry were changed when he felt his heart 'strangely warmed').

3. Ian Petit, a Christian author, maintains that we are combustible, and that the Holy Spirit is the spark who ignites us. But we keep pouring on water. What makes us afraid? (Draw out different fears the group might have, some perhaps based on negative personal experiences. Don't spend too much time on this.)

4. How do we receive the Holy Spirit? Read John 14: 15–17. (As we choose Jesus, he gives us the gift of the Holy Spirit who enables us to continue to grow in our love for him. It is important to demystify the Holy Spirit somewhat; we need to make him welcome, be hospitable to him, for he's an invited guest.)

5. What is the difference between the gift of the Holy Spirit and the gifts of the Holy Spirit? Read John 16: 5–15; 1 Corinthians 12:4–11. (Take each passage and discuss it for a few minutes. The first passage tells us

what the Holy Spirit will do for us individually and corporately, whereas the second passage tells us about specific gifts and how they operate within the Church.)

6. Look at 1 Corinthians 12:4–11 again. Try to put the gifts in the following categories: gifts of speech, gifts of practical ministry, gifts of 'working wonders'. How are these gifts used in your daily life and in the life of the Church? (Here is a structure which may help your group classify the gifts:

(a) Gifts of speech – prophecy, instruction, speaking in tongues and interpreting tongues.

(b) Gifts of practical ministry – care for the needy, serving, encouraging, contributing, acts of mercy and administration.

(c) Gifts of 'working wonders' – healing and performing miracles. Continue to refer to the 1 Corinthians passage. Encourage the group to see that they have been empowered by the Holy Spirit to do the things that they have already been doing. You may need to emphasise the practical ministry area (see (b) above) first.

Ask if members have experienced any of the gifts listed under (a) and (c), and what it was like. Try to draw out positive experiences from possible negative ones. Those who have had negative experiences may have thrown the baby out with the dirty bath-water. One good rule of thumb is to remember that the Holy Spirit will always bring order and give glory to Christ. He will also always be true to Scripture.

Be sure to acknowledge that this is just an introduction, and that there will no be time to go into an in-depth discussion on each gift listed. If people express interest, they should be referred to others who may be able to give them further instruction.)

7. What is the fruit of the Spirit? Read Galatians 5:22–5.
8. Which do you think are more important, the fruit of the Spirit or the gifts of the Spirit? Why?
9. Can we identify the fruit of the Spirit at work in our own and others' lives? (Draw out the key points from discussion of question 3 and build on this.)

To close

1. Share or sum up what has actually been learnt, especially that we all need the Holy Spirit.
2. Pray. Ask everyone to join in the prayer 'The Fire of Love'.

THE FIRE OF LOVE

Come to us Holy Spirit as you came
    to the apostles.
Open our minds that we may see
    the hidden things of God.
Send love into our hearts like a
    Flame of Fire.
That our lives may be changed by
    the power of your Spirit.
To do God's work on earth and
    bring people with us to
    heaven.

AMEN.

Continue in prayer, asking that the Holy Spirit will indeed fill you all. Ask the group to close their eyes and imagine that they are a cup. Ask each to open their hands to symbolise being an empty vessel. Imagine that the cup is being filled from the bottom to top, then overflowing. Allow a few minutes, then close by thanking the Holy Spirit for his gentle touch, his presence with you.

Close by all saying together the grace as follows:

May the grace we have received
  Lord,
Sink deeply within our hearts,
Bear fruit in our lives;
Keep us always in thanksgiving
In praise of your Name.

          AMEN.

SESSION 6 – THE CHURCH

We believe in one holy catholic and
  apostolic Church.
We acknowledge one baptism for the
  forgiveness of sins.
We look for the resurrection of the dead,
and the life of the world to come.

          AMEN.

Key learning points

1. Practical understanding of the Church.
2. Putting into action the words 'holy, catholic and apostolic'.

Welcome

Take care of any practical details and introduce the study.

Pray

A brief prayer that the group may be strong in their membership of the Church and active on God's behalf.

Bible texts that could be studied

John 17:22–3; 1 Peter 2:9; Revelation 7:9; Acts 2:42–7; Matthew 26:26–8; John 13:34–6; Ephesians 4:11–13.

Questions to stimulate discussion

(Allow 50–60 minutes)

1. What do we mean by 'Church'? (Invite the members

to discuss their thoughts. You might want to use paper to summarise their ideas, perhaps drawing in question 2 below and using a different pen colour to help people see the contrasts. This might be referred to again when you come to question 3c.)

2. What do your friends and neighbours think the Church is? (Challenge members to consider others' views who are not Christians, or those who seldom attend services.)

3. What are the characteristics of the Church we are members of? What do we say in the Creed?
   (a) It should be *one*. Read John 17:22–3. What are some of the obstacles to unity?
   (b) It should be *holy*. Read 1 Peter 2:9. We talked in an earlier session about God being holy. What makes the Church holy?
   (c) It should be *catholic*, i.e. open to all. Read Revelation 7:9. Is your church open to everyone? If not, why not? (Do different types of people seem to feel uncomfortable in your church? How are new people welcomed? Do they keep coming back?)
   (d) It should be *apostolic*. Read Acts 2:42–7. 'Apostolic' means behaving like the Apostles did. What did they do? Let's look at the early apostolic church. (They were devoted to teaching, to the fellowship, to breaking of bread and prayer. They gave as people had need, met together regularly, ate together regularly, had sincere hearts and praised God. Signs and wonders followed and the Lord added to their numbers daily.)

4. How do we, as individuals, fit into the body of the Church, the 'communion of saints', the community of believers? What do the following passages say to us?
   (a) Matthew 26:26–8. (Draw out the mystery of being part of, or sharing in, Christ's Body.)
   (b) John 13:34–5. (Our greatest testimony to the

world happens when Christ's love in us enables us
to love one another.)
- (c) Ephesians 4:11–17. (Draw out our uniqueness,
diversity of gifts, work of the Spirit to bring unity
and direction.)
5. Identify one particular area of your church which
could be changed in a positive way. Think through
how this could be done. What will be your part in this?
Can you let your church leaders know about this?

Pray

Ask members to pray for the needs of their church.

To close

Say the Grace together. Encourage the members to keep
their eyes open, speaking out the words to one another.

THE GRACE

May the grace of our Lord Jesus Christ,
and the love of God,
and the fellowship of the Holy Spirit,
be with us all evermore.

AMEN.

(2 Corinthians 13:14)

SESSION 7 – GO OUT INTO THE WORLD

Key learning points

1. To apply what we have learned:
   - (a) as individuals,
   - (b) as a group,
   - (c) as a parish.
2. That evangelism is our responsibility.

Welcome

Take care of any practical details and introduce the study. Remind the participants that this is the last study of this series.

Pray

A brief prayer that the group may be faithful servants and witnesses.

Bible texts that could be used

Matthew 28:19,20; Matthew 25:31–46; 2 Corinthians 4:13–15.

Questions to stimulate discussion
(Allow 50–60 minutes)

1. Read Matthew 28:19–20. Jesus is speaking to the disciples. Do you consider yourself a disciple? What does being a disciple mean to you? (Elements include learning, loving, accepting, following, obeying, growing. Can members remember times when they have experienced these practical demonstrations of discipleship?)

2. Jesus said, 'I am with you always'. Reflect back to times in your life when you have been aware of his presence. Can you identify some of those individuals or groups who have helped in your growth as a disciple? How did they represent Jesus? (Often we do not recognise that Jesus' presence is within individuals or groups who affect our lives. We ourselves often don't know when we are representing Jesus. Each is an example of being a disciple.)

3. Read Matthew 25:31–46. If God is in the hungry, the thirsty, the naked, the stranger, the sick and the prisoner, what should be our response? (Acknowledge that this is an overwhelming list and that we don't have an individual responsibility for all these groups. We should, however, see our gifts used in our com-

munity as we support one another in our particular ministries. And we also have a responsibility in the wider world to be informed, concerned, and then take action.)

4. Is this evangelism? (We evangelise by what we say and do, as well as who we are. Do we tend to view the witness of 'who we are' as secondary to what we do? Which of the two is probably the more profound?)

5. Many people are concerned, compassionate. What makes the Christian disciple different? (We are not saying that Christians do it better, or that we have nothing to gain from secular skills and training. The difference is that we recognise the lordship of Christ; we have a Gospel to proclaim.)

6. Read 2 Corinthians 4:13–15. Can you identify opportunities for speaking about your faith? Do these occur when we are helping others? If so, can you share an example? (Try to get the group to share some common experiences they have had, everyday situations where they were able to share with someone, or be a witness.)

7. What should we do as a church? What should we be as a church? How can we create opportunities to introduce the enquirer to the worshipping community? (Begin by asking what the church usually does when newcomers attend the services – how are they drawn into the fellowship? Are they able to feel part of it? How can we encourage people to come to church? Has anyone been in this situation? If not, how could the group begin to reach out?)

8. Where can we get help so that we can be more effective disciples? What resources are available in our parish, in our town, in our diocese? (Ask the group about things that might be happening in the parish; can someone share about these?)

Pray

Begin by reminding the members that this is the last group, and perhaps it would be a good time to thank the Lord for special experiences and things which have happened during the time together as a group. Allow time for those who wish to share to do so. Close the time with the Grace, said with eyes open, sharing it with one another.

We Believe – Exploring and Living the Creed Today: Group Leaders' Training Course

We suggest that parishes who wish to use the 'We Believe' course send prospective group leaders on a short training course to equip them to lead the material. It is helpful for prospective group leaders to attend a training weekend so that they can 'catch the vision' behind the course and also experience some of the material.

Before exploring the nature and structure of the training weekend it may be useful to explain the main motives behind the preparation of the 'We Believe' course. The Nicene Creed was chosen because its content is a summary of the major doctrines of the Church, and is acceptable to all the various Christian traditions. The aim of the course is to deepen participants' understanding of their faith and to do this in an enjoyable and mutually supportive atmosphere. The approach used involves participation of all members of the group and does not require group leaders to be teachers but rather facilitators who set the atmosphere for the group meetings and guide members through the material. In the past few years many churches have experienced the benefits of attending small groups on a regular basis. Within a warm and accepting environment friendships are formed, and people are given the opportunity to discuss their faith together and to deepen their understanding and experience. It has become evident that more churches would like to start running such groups but feel that they would benefit from some assistance regarding training leaders and providing appropriate material.

It is against this background that the 'We Believe' course was prepared. The seven sessions of the course involve an exploration of the Creed. It is hoped that participation in the 'We Believe' course will increase group members' confidence as far as sharing their faith is concerned. This is clearly a matter of real importance when considering the effectiveness of the Decade of Evangelism.

In the Blackburn diocese the Group Leaders' Training Weekend takes place on a Friday evening between 7.30 p.m. and 9.15 p.m. and on Saturday between 9.30 a.m. and 3.15 p.m. On page 116 is an example of a typical programme. The majority of the training takes place in groups and for every eight to ten course members there are two course leaders. Course members are split randomly into groups after the introduction on the Friday evening and they remain in the same groups throughout the weekend. An ideal group size is ten including the two leaders, with twelve being an absolute maximum. The two leaders share leadership of the group and lead different sessions.

The Friday evening commences with a general welcome and basic explanation of the format for the weekend and then members of the leadership team are briefly introduced. It is essential that right from the beginning of the weekend a warm, relaxed and friendly atmosphere is established.

It is also crucial that everyone is encouraged to have a sense of expectation that God will speak to them during the weekend both through the material and through listening to each other. After a prayer committing the weekend to the Lord and asking the Holy Spirit to speak, members go into their groups for approximately one and a quarter hours. It is important that everyone speaks and hears the sound of their own voice during the first few minutes of the group session and to this end individuals are invited to introduce themselves to the other members of the group by giving their name and three pieces of information about family, jobs or hobbies. Although some people find this quite 'nerve-wracking' everyone tends to feel better and more relaxed once they have made their contribution. After these introductions the group works through Session 1 of the 'We Believe' course, entitled 'In the beginning'. One of the leaders takes prime responsibility for leading the session but is assisted by the other co-leader. This model of shared leadership is important because when the 'We Believe' course is done in parishes each group is led by two co-leaders. Each group therefore has the experience of two different leadership styles and personalities and the approach tends to prevent one leader being seen as the expert or teacher.

After the session has been completed time is left for group members to discuss the material they have just experienced, and to share with one another how it feels to be in a group with people one does not know well.

All groups come together for the final quarter of an hour when practical issues regarding the following day are dealt with. There is an opportunity here for any questions to be asked. It is important to finish on time.

After a brief welcome and opening prayer, course members go straight into their groups on the Saturday morning and work through Session 2 of the course, entitled 'Meekness and majesty'. Prior to doing this it is useful to do another 'icebreaker'. For instance, group members could be invited to tell the group another three things about themselves, but this time one should be untrue.

Can the group come to a consensus as to which piece of

information is false? This exercise, lasting perhaps fifteen minutes, is usually extremely enjoyable and gives rise to much laughter, getting the day off to a good start. It is normal for the second group leader to lead the material on this occasion. After this session course members come together again for a fifteen-minute slot looking at practical issues. Here, discussion can take place on issues which need to be decided before starting off leading a parish housegroup. The main questions to be considered briefly here are: where? when? how often? how many group members? You also need to think about timing. After a fifteen-minute coffee-break all course members come back together for another short fifteen-minute session looking at how people often feel when they attend a housegroup for the first time. The Four I's stand for Insecurity, Ignorance, Insignificance, and Inability, and they are used to encourage people to explore the feelings they commonly experience in new and unfamiliar surroundings.

Immediately after this session, course members go back into their groups and work through Session 5 of the 'We Believe' course, entitled 'The life-giving Spirit'. There should be plenty of time left towards the end of this section to enable the group to share in a time of prayer led by the group leader. It is essential that as well as talking about the Holy Spirit, opportunity is given for people to open up and be filled with the Spirit. The experience of this session is very important. People are encouraged to believe that God will equip them for group leadership ministry, and it is important that they are given the opportunity to receive from him. The session concludes with a prayer of thanksgiving in which all members participate.

By the end of this third session most groups will have bonded well together, and the time of prayer will usually be powerful and moving. After a lunch break, all course members meet together for the concluding session. It is good to look together at the qualities that are needed to lead a group well. Sometimes it is helpful to split course members into groups of four or five and ask them to identify what they consider to be the most important characteristics of a good group leader. Alternatively, this activity could be done by means of a group 'brainstorming session'. No one has all the ideal qualities, but it is useful to identify the most important qualities necessary.

In the final session course members are given time to share any concerns or questions that they have in an open question and answer/discussion session. The concluding activity is to split people into their parish teams so that they can make practical plans regarding starting a group, or groups, in their parish.

After, sometimes, initial apprehension most people enjoy the fact that the course involves a lot of participation and little passivity. This is of course the model they will use back in their parishes. People find it very useful to have experienced such a substantial part of the course before leading it for others. Overwhelmingly, people find this approach preferable to being told about the course and how to lead it. Of course people cannot be trained to be good group leaders in such a short time, and in fact there is obviously very little formal input about such things as group dynamics and leadership techniques. The main hope is that people go away having 'caught the vision' and feeling excited and encouraged about leading the course in their parish. If people have experienced God speaking to them in the Training Course they will then see the potential for this to continue. Most people greatly enjoy the opportunity of learning and sharing together in a friendly and informal atmosphere, and can take this experience back to their parishes, enabling other people to participate in the course and enjoy the same benefits. Such participation in the course encourages people to be less self-conscious in talking about their faith and gives the added motivation and confidence to do so whenever appropriate. The Gospel is very much worth sharing!

We Believe – Exploring and Living the Creed Today:
Group Leaders' Training Course

SUGGESTED PROGRAMME

FRIDAY EVENING

7.15	Arrival and tea/coffee
7.30– 7.40 p.m.	Welcome
7.40– 7.45 p.m.	Team introduction
7.45– 9.00 p.m.	Small groups
	SESSION 1: In the beginning
9.00– 9.15 p.m.	Practical issues for Saturday

SATURDAY

9.15– 9.30 a.m.	Tea/coffee
	Welcome prayer
9.30–10.45 a.m.	Small groups
	SESSION 2: Meekness and majesty
10.45–11.00 a.m.	Practical issues in small groups
11.00–11.15 a.m.	Break
11.15–11.30 a.m.	Four I's, in groups
11.30–12.45 p.m.	Small groups
	SESSION 5: The life-giving Spirit
12.45– 1.30 p.m.	Lunch
1.30– 2.15 p.m.	Small groups
	Characteristics of group leaders
	Concerns leaders share
2.15– 2.45 p.m.	Getting started in your church – dividing into church teams to plan
2.45– 3.15 p.m.	Team available for individual questions

Preparing for a Parish Mission

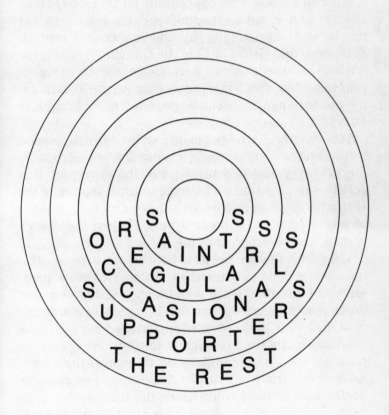

The above diagram is not so much a target as simply a number of concentric circles like those made when a stone is dropped into a pool. The diagram illustrates the well-known fact that in our journey towards God each of us tends to move one circle at a time; it is a long process. Few people jump from the outside to the centre in one leap; even if this appears to be the case, the preparation and movement for this leap is still there, though hidden.

A parish mission is the opportunity for everyone to take another step, to move into another circle. It is directed at regular and long-standing church members just as much as to those completely outside the church. It is about the renewal of the church; it is about the recovery of priorities; it is about the preparation of the church for mission to its parish. '*In mission the church is always speaking to itself.*'

This chapter describes the one style of parish mission the author has experience in leading. It is not necessarily the best way and is definitely not the only way. It is certainly not a substitute for the continual sharing of the faith with those around which is the continuing life-blood of any church. It is simply a period when the church emphasises this aspect of its life.

The parish mission needs to be well prepared for. This implies a period of not usually less than two years' preparation beginning with wide-ranging discussion and much prayer before the decision is made and a preacher is invited. The style of mission outlined here is quite traditional, centering on nightly mission services with a preacher who is able under God to express the Gospel truths profoundly yet simply. The wrong preacher can undo years of good work! Once the decision has been made and a preacher invited, a group of people needs to be chosen, and each one given a particular responsibility in preparation for the mission. There follows an outline of the responsibilities involved.

(1) Prayer

The whole enterprise must be undergirded by prayer and someone needs to take on the responsibility of making sure that this happens. This means, among other things, the writing of many letters to, for example, religious communities, asking for their prayers. It means encouraging members of the congregation to contact their Christian friends and churches with which they may be connected with the same request. The replies to all this correspondence are displayed in church to encourage the faithful by the knowledge that they are being prayed for.

The person responsible for prayer will also make sure that individuals are asked to pray for the mission, possibly through the development of a personal prayer card which they are asked to use daily and/or in prayer triplets or small groups. This part of the preparation for the mission has often been the beginning of the formation of a regular parish prayer group. It cannot be emphasised too strongly that parish missions stand or fall by the seriousness with which prayer is taken as part of the preparations.

(2) Publicity

The person responsible for publicity needs to have a certain flair and may gather together a group of others who may or may not be connected with the church but who are gifted in the presentation of publicity and communication materials. In this way the mission itself begins by attracting the time and skills of those who otherwise may be little involved in the life of the church. The mission is often to them as well as being through them. This group will be responsible for making sure that everyone in the parish is aware of just what is going on and why. This will be done through letters, posters, leaflets, local radio and any other means at their disposal.

(3) **The team**

During the mission itself the preacher will bring with him or her a team of men and women, old and young, lay and ordained, whose function will be outlined later in the chapter. At an early stage this team needs to be chosen and someone needs to keep in touch with them.

(4) **Hosts**

Someone has to be responsible for the provision of bed and breakfast for the members of the visiting team and also for organising an evening meal in a different house each evening for every member of the team. This can be a logistical nightmare!

(5) **Catering**

The mission team has lunch together each day and usually needs to be provided with a constant supply of coffee.

(6) **Visiting**

A parish mission is an ideal opportunity for every house in the parish to be contacted by the church. In many churches this is the least popular activity in preparation for a mission. Most people are willing to do anything exept knock on doors and so this must be made as easy as possible. The parish is divided into areas and every house in each area receives a letter announcing that a visit will be made from the parish church about the mission which will take place in a few weeks' time. The visitors go two by two and simply invite the occupants of each house to attend a mission service offering to call for anyone who would prefer not to come alone, and also offering the opportunity of a visit by a member of the team during the mission itself should they wish to talk about the Christian faith. Usually more than five per cent of households accept the offer of a visit by the team and this forms the basis for their work during the mission. The congregation having visited every house saves time for the team but also makes contacts for the parish. The clergy and their experienced lay Christians accompany the visitors and 'loiter with intent', should any of the visitors feel out of their depth and need some sort of back-up.

(7) Treasurer (8) Secretary (9) Chairman/woman
Each of these are necessary members of the working party but their particular functions do not need to be discussed here.

This group will meet monthly for not less than a year before the mission itself. It is important that about a year before the mission every member of the congregation is informed, either by letter or by being invited to a meeting or both, of all the jobs that need to be done, and volunteers acquired.

Suggested Timetable for the Mission

SAT. p.m.		Team arrive; team meeting
SUN. a.m.		Commissioning
p.m.		Guest service/event
MON.–FRI.	7.00 a.m.	Eucharist
	8.30 a.m.	Morning prayer (school assemblies)
		Time available for silence
	10.00 a.m.	Team meeting
	12.00	Eucharist
	1.00 p.m.	Lunch (together)
	2.00 p.m.	Visiting (4.00 p.m. children)
	5.00 p.m.	Evening prayer
	6.00 p.m.	Supper
	7.30 p.m.	Mission service & coffee/ visiting
SAT.		Free/social
SUN. a.m.		Usual Sunday services
p.m.		Guest service/event

MON.–WED.   As above
THURS. 7.00 a.m.   Eucharist

Mission begins.

The mission service each evening should be simple and informal, lasting no longer than an hour and focusing particularly on an address which communicates what is at the heart of the Gospel.

Suggested themes for the services might be:

1. Who am I?
2. What is God like?
3. Jesus calls.
4. Jesus heals.
5. Jesus died.
6. Jesus lives.
7. What use is the Church?
8. What about me?

Every parish is different and therefore every mission has its own local variations. Some include extra work with young children and/or work in schools. Some include housegroups, others don't. What has been suggested above is simply one outline and is open to a variety of interpretations.

The outcome of a parish mission is God's business and it is a profound mistake to be too particular about follow-up. We must be ready for whatever God intends and not make decisions on his behalf. Generally numbers do not increase dramatically, certainly in the initial stages, but the church is always renewed and deepened. A parish mission can be seen as a preparation for mission, it must never be seen as an end but always more of a beginning.

The parish should be ready towards the end of the mission to listen carefully to what God is encouraging the church to become and to do. It has often been the case that immediately following the mission, prayer groups, study groups, 'Know your Faith' classes, pastoral visiting teams, quiet days and retreats have started. Most parishes look back on their parish mission as a new beginning and often most particularly for those who have been involved in the church for many years. None of us has arrived! God's mission is always to me. Maybe the best testimony comes from a lady in the parish that hosted the first mission at which one of the authors preached: as she put it, 'What used to be a duty is now a joy'.

(J.N.)

Spiritual Direction

Am I Too Loud? is the title of the autobiography of Gerald Moore who was probably the most famous piano accompanist of his time. His was a special art; by his playing he enabled the very best to come from those whom he accompanied. He did not get in the way by playing too loud yet he was indispensable to the performer's art. An accompanist accompanies. In other words he gets alongside those whom he seeks to help.

A spiritual director, soul friend – there are many names more or less appropriate to the task – is essentially an accompanist. Many of us are convinced that we need a companion for our spiritual journey, some of us feel called to be one for others.

The first and most important thing to remember about spiritual direction is that there is only one spiritual director and that is the Holy Spirit. Our task is simply not to get in the way of that direction. This is more easily said than done for the spiritual director can be both dangerous and powerful having access as he or she does to the inmost secrets of another person's heart. If we do not know ourselves well enough, if we do not know our need of God, if we are in the habit of passing judgement on others or of looking down on others then we are certain to get in the way and should avoid this ministry. Remember always that the Gospel is good news, and this is an affirming ministry.

A spiritual director is there to help us in bad times and good. It is not just about problem solving nor indeed is it just about the forgiveness of sins. Regularity of meeting is therefore more important than frequency. If meetings only take place when there are problems to be solved then growth does not take place, at best we return to the status quo.

The relationship between the individual and his or her spiritual director is a precious one. Total trust and total confidentiality are of the essence in this relationship. We must never keep anything off the agenda, we must try together under the guidance of the Holy Spirit to look for causes rather than symptoms; there must be warmth, generosity and love in the relationship; this means that there will be vulnerability too. A good spiritual director will never indulge our failings but will always be gentle in admonition.

Many are afraid of exposing their inner selves to another person in this way for fear that the other may think less of them as a result. It is well attested that this is never the case. When someone opens their heart to another under the guidance of the Holy Spirit the love between them is deepened and increased.

One thing to come out of this relationship may well be a *rule of life*. We all need disciplines, structures and safety nets in our everyday life, and it is no less so in our relationship with God. However, there is a danger that a rule of life can become an ideal which we seek to attain yet never achieve and the result is simply the breeding of more guilt. A rule of life should always be attainable in normal circumstances. When it is broken it could be seen as a warning sign that personal discipline is beginning to slip. A rule of life should not only include a discipline about prayer and Bible study, but should cover every aspect of our life, for example time spent with family, use of money and work. It is as well after working out an initial rule to try it for six months, and after that revise it each year (maybe on one's annual retreat).

Finally, the spiritual director may also act as confessor. Again when properly understood this sacrament is not the prerogative, outside the Roman Catholic Church, of a few Anglo-Catholics. It is a joyful sacrament of assurance of the forgiveness of sins. We sin against God and against each other, and the priest as he or she listens to us represents all our brothers and sisters in Christ whom we have offended. In their name and in God's name he or she assures us of that forgiveness which is already there. For many of us confession is an essential part of the ministry of healing and reconciliation which is so integral to the good news of the Gospel.

(J.N.)

Retreats

Jesus, during his earthly ministry, found it necessary to spend time alone with his Father. It was when he was alone in the wilderness that he was tempted. It was when he was alone in Gethsemane that he suffered the pain of yielding his will to the Father's. It was when he was alone that he could rest awhile and be strengthened for ministry. If being alone with the Father was necessary to Jesus, must it not be so with us? This is what a retreat is: time alone with God. We make time (usually a weekend or the inside of a week); we leave behind the normal activities of life; we usually (though not always) go away to a quiet place (monastery, convent or retreat house). We may simply spend the time alone joining in the worship of the community where we are staying as we feel appropriate (private retreat). We may spend some time with someone who will help us to enter into the retreat more effectively and accompany us on our journey (individually directed retreat) or we may, alongside others, be helped by someone who gives a series of retreat addresses (preached retreat). But these are only the externals and are there to help the real retreat happen, to help free us from distractions, to be alone with God. We need to go into retreat with minds and hearts open to whatever God would have in store for us. What happens must be left to him, he knows what he is about. A retreat may be a time of rest, peace, joy and intimate fellowship with God.

On the other hand, as for Jesus, it may be a time of deep temptation, of suffering, of emptiness, of a sense only of the absence of God rather than his presence. Whatever a retreat brings we must understand that God knows what he is about, he knows what is best for us.

The retreat movement has grown immensely in recent years. There was a time when it was thought that only those of an Anglo-Catholic persuasion went on retreat. Thankfully this is no longer the case. Retreats are not about a particular type of churchmanship, they are for anyone who takes their spiritual journey seriously.

Most people in our society live faster and more super-ficial lives than at any time in our history. This means that both the need for retreat is greater and yet at the same time it is more difficult to leave behind the external noise and busyness of everyday life. For most of us it is more difficult than ever to be not just with God but with ourselves. Most of us have something of a history of running away from God and ourselves but at the end of the day this is a fruitless exercise (if you do not believe that read Psalm 139). The need for retreat has never been greater, because it builds the depth necessary to sustain the increasing demands made on us as Christians in the twentieth century.

(J.N.)